In *Rivers of Delight,* Dick Eastman opens our eyes to the amazing possibilities associated with deep, sincere, humble worship and challenges us to "take the plunge" into the river of God's blessing that overflows its banks. I encourage you to jump into this book with both feet!

BILL MCCARTNEY
FOUNDER AND PRESIDENT, PROMISE KEEPERS

In *Rivers of Delight,* Dick Eastman uniquely focuses on the tributaries converging in the Church to fashion the river of worship, prayer and world evangelization. The emergence of biblically focused worship is a fountainhead where the life within the Church and within the individual moves from flow to overflow. As we exalt Jesus Christ, Dick challenges us to call on God's authority to eliminate the adversary's position as nations are brought to their knees in a feast of joy. The culmination of the Great Commission will be ushered in on the foundation of anticipatory, prayerful worship that brings us to the destiny God intended for each of His people.

TOM PHILLIPS
VICE PRESIDENT OF TRAINING,
BILLY GRAHAM EVANGELISTIC ASSOCIATION

How refreshing it was to cruise the 10 rivers of delight in Dick Eastman's new book on intercessory worship. Dick's practical, personal intercessory prayer life, his solid biblical foundation and his years of international ministry have blended to give us a captivating book of hope. Hope in the sense that we will live to see the Earth filled with the knowledge of the glory of the Lord!

EDDIE SMITH
FOUNDER AND PRESIDENT, U.S. PRAYER CENTER

RIVERS

of

DELIGHT

RIVERS

of

DELIGHT

DICK EASTMAN

Regal

From Gospel Light
Ventura, California, U.S.A.

Published by Regal Books
From Gospel Light
Ventura, California, U.S.A.
Printed in the U.S.A.

Rights for publishing this book in other languages are contracted by
Gospel Light Worldwide, the international nonprofit ministry of
Gospel Light. Gospel Light Worldwide also provides publishing and
technical assistance to international publishers dedicated to producing
Sunday School and Vacation Bible School curricula and books in
the languages of the world. For additional information, visit
www.gospellightworldwide.org; write to Gospel Light Worldwide,
P.O. Box 3875, Ventura, CA 93006; or send an
e-mail to info@gospellightworldwide.org.

CONTENTS

LET THE RIVERS FLOW

All humanity finds shelter in the shadow of your wings.
You feed them from the abundance of your own house, letting
them drink from your rivers of delight.

PSALM 36:7-8, *NLT*

This book was born September 11, 2001. It is a date Americans will always remember. Several weeks prior to this now infamous day of devastating terrorist attacks on America, I had finished the first two books of my *Delight* trilogy—*Heights of*

13

Delight and *Pathways of Delight*. I decided to travel to California from Colorado on September 10 to meet with the publishers of the trilogy, Regal Books, the following morning. We were to discuss how the three titles might be released.

Focused on the emerging theme of intercessory worship (increasingly identified with the harp and bowl symbols of Revelation 5:8), two of the manuscripts were complete; but all I had for the third was a concept, with several case studies to support it, and a title—*Rivers of Delight.*

For several years I have observed a growing recognition of prophetic ministry in the Body of Christ and, more recently, prophetic worship—something I will define shortly. Here I will simply say that I saw rivers of passionate prophetic worship along with fervent, focused intercession beginning to flow throughout the Church globally. I was convinced healing for the nations would arise with prophetic worship.

Eighteen months earlier, on the first day of what was to become a 40-day worship fast (described in the first book of my trilogy, *Heights of Delight*), God had drawn my attention to Psalm 37:4 and the familiar promise that He would give those who delight in Him the desires of their heart. During the first moments of that fast, I felt God inviting me to new "heights of delight" in Him. I had already determined I would set aside the following 40 days for fasting and prayer (something I had done only once before in my life), but that first day God was impressing on my heart that this fast would be different. It was to be a season of *fasting and worship,* not just *fasting and prayer.* I was to turn all my prayer times daily, for the full 40 days, into seasons of intercessory worship by *singing* all of my praise and prayer.

Again that day, as I opened my Bible to Psalm 37:4 to read the beauty of this promise of delighting in God, my eyes caught a glimpse of a phrase in the previous Psalm. It read, "All humanity finds shelter in the shadow of your wings. You feed them from the abundance of your own house, letting them drink from your rivers of delight" (Ps. 36:7-8, *NLT*).

In subsequent days, as this worship-fast unfolded, the phrase "rivers of delight" filled my mind. What were the rivers? What did it mean to drink from them? How could we release them? The several unique descriptions of life-giving rivers in Scripture immediately came to mind (as I describe in chapter one), as well as how the rivers are associated with God's intimate presence and His desire to heal. I felt God saying that He had many "rivers of delight" that would someday flow through His people out to the entire world. In those rivers we would see the literal transformation of nations.

These thoughts were on my mind as I flew to California late Monday, September 10, for my meeting with the editors the following morning. While I was hesitant to discuss that book three was merely a concept, I was encouraged that the manuscripts for books one and two were complete.

I awakened September 11 just after 6:30 A.M., PST. My usual custom upon awakening when I travel is to turn on the television to catch the news before stepping into the shower. I flipped the television on, not expecting or prepared for what I was about to see.

It all seemed so confusing. I thought I had tuned to a news channel but it appeared I had selected a movie channel by mistake as a giant jet airliner flew into one of the twin towers of New York City's World Trade Center. *Those special effects are good*, I thought, as I reached for the remote to change to a news channel. But suddenly the familiar face of a well-known journalist uttered, "What you are seeing is *live*. America is under attack by terrorists."

I sat up in the bed, stunned. Then the footage jumped to a second jetliner, flying at full speed—slam—into the other tower. Soon I would watch in horror, together with millions of other people around the world, the two 110-story towers implode, collapsing like old buildings intentionally demolished, straight down in a cloud of dust.

Ninety minutes later my meeting with the editors went on as scheduled, though on an obviously somber note. It was understandably difficult to concentrate under the circumstances. Still, we discussed release plans for all three books as a series in the upcoming year, 2002. My plan was to fly home that afternoon, but I soon learned that all flights across America had been grounded. This had never happened in America's aviation history. I was stranded.

As my meeting with the editors concluded, I had little idea I would be there seven more days. I decided to make the best of it, so that first afternoon I began praying about the content of book three—*Rivers of Delight*. In prayer, my concept quickly gave way to something more substantive.

I envisioned an array of prophetic, supernatural rivers being released through God's people. The channel that carried the rivers was prophetic intercessory worship. I was convinced that these rivers would flow out of the harp and bowl intercessory worship movement, a movement I introduced in *Heights of Delight* and *Pathways of Delight*. This movement, based on the symbolism of Revelation 5:8-10 that depicts heavenly worshipers holding harps (symbolic of worship) and bowls (symbolic of intercession), is growing rapidly and sowing seeds of transformation throughout the world.

On the pages that follow I will provide an overview of various prophetic dimensions of intercessory worship and each dimension's corresponding supernatural river that releases God's presence and power wherever it flows. These "rivers of delight" are indeed beckoning us to come and drink freely. Let the rivers flow.

> Let the poor man say,
> "I am rich in Him."
> Let the lost man say,
> "I am found in Him."
> Let the river flow.
>
> Let the blind man say,
> "I can see again."
> Let the dead man say,
> "I am born again."
> Let the river flow,
> Let the river flow.[1]

MAKE ROOM FOR MY GLORY

RIVER OF INTIMACY: THE PROPHETIC DIMENSION OF INTERCESSORY WORSHIP

For the tenth time God whispered in my heart, "Make room for My glory."

I knew it was the tenth time because I was counting. It was now past midnight, and I had little hope of sleep. I had no idea I would soon be introduced to the realm of prophetic response in worship. I was not into many "prophetic" concepts or ideas at that point in my life, and I doubt I had ever heard the term "prophetic worship" prior to this experience.

My journey into this dimension of worship actually began several months earlier when I was invited to speak at a conference in Texas for a large gathering of university students. More than 5,000 college-aged youth were expected, representing almost every major university in America, as well as several overseas universities. I was surprised to be invited, especially when I saw the list of 10 other speakers—all of whom were well known. Most had radio or television ministries and were highly regarded conference speakers.

I was asked to lead several smaller prayer gatherings in the afternoons during the conference, as well as speak in three plenary sessions. A hotel ballroom had been reserved for this purpose. The organizers warned me in advance that those participating might be small in number but that it was vital to provide a prayer covering over the conference. I was honored to accept the invitation.

WHISPERS IN THE NIGHT

For my plenary sessions I prepared three related teachings

with worksheets, each building on the previous lesson. The overall theme was "How to Be a Prayer Mobilizer." Lessons one and two were introductory to the third, which I felt was the most important lesson. Lesson three's worksheets included the "how to" portion of the teaching, a detail that I emphasize because of God's repeated whispers in the night to me—"Make room for My glory!"

I was excited about these messages because I felt students could use the information to mobilize others to pray when they returned to their campuses. I also realized I would have a captive audience because everyone was required to attend all three plenary meetings. I felt that as I built one lesson upon the other, these 5,000 student leaders would be better equipped to be mobilizers of prayer.

To spark interest, I intentionally distributed all three worksheets in the first session rather than handing out one sheet per session. I wanted to whet the students' appetites for further teaching by showing them the various outlines.

Following the first lesson I was encouraged by the increase in the number of students who attended the optional prayer meetings. From a handful the first day, attendance increased to 200 the second day. On the third

CHAPTER ONE

day the number increased even more.

The following morning would be my final plenary session, and I was to be the first of the various speakers. That third night God would visit me in a most peculiar way. But before that, there was something unique He would show me that afternoon.

The prayer time was scheduled to last two hours. After a few introductory moments we were seeking God. Then, about an hour into the gathering, I felt an impression to move from my kneeling position to lying prostrate before the Lord.

For almost one hour I lay in that position. Soon I began to weep, and I could hear others weeping as well. A deep brokenness was settling in the room.

A WOMB OF GLORY

Finally I sat up and looked around—amazed. Every person was on his or her face in prayer without any direction from me. I felt the Lord speak, "This is a womb of My glory."

A womb, of course, is where life is conceived. It is from a womb where life is finally birthed into its fullness.

An impression followed, *What you see here today I long to do for the entire group tomorrow. I desire to transform the entire convention center into a womb of My glory.*

I prayerfully thought, *That sounds nice, Lord, but how is it possible?*

This was one of those prayer questions for which an immediate answer was not necessarily expected. I even wondered if I were imagining all this. And how could what happened so spontaneously with just a few hundred people happen in a highly organized plenary setting with thousands of people? The more I thought about it, the more I concluded it was just wishful thinking. What my mind kept coming back to was my final message for that next morning. But first there would be that long, sleepless night.

THE WHISPERS OF GOD

As Dee and I retired for the night, I am sure my wife sensed my restlessness. Yet, as is customary for Dee, she was deeply sleeping in seconds while I tossed and turned.

Sleep was not to be. I tried everything. I am sure I counted both sheep and blessings until I lost count of what I was counting. Finally I asked the Lord, "Why can't I sleep when I face such an important assignment?"

And that is when I first heard God's whisper, "Make room for My glory!"

I responded, "God, is that You?"

I heard the words again, "Make room for My glory!"

"How, God? What do you mean?" I asked.

He answered with the same statement, "Make room for My glory!"

I asked, "How can I make room for Your glory?" I really had no idea what God wanted me to do.

After hearing the same impression 10 times, I desperately said, "Okay, God! Whatever it means, I will do it!"

I still had no idea what God wanted me to do, but He seemed to honor my small step of faith. Suddenly He asked, "Have you ever heard finer Bible teaching than you've heard these past two days?"

I was not sure where this was going, but I said, "No, Lord, I can't remember being more inspired by teaching than at this gathering." It was, indeed, some of the best I had ever heard.

"Have you ever experienced more zealous and joyful music than among these college youth?" the Lord asked.

I answered, "Never, Lord." Then I added, "These students radiate zeal!"

"There's only one problem," He said firmly. "In all of this activity, no one has taken the time to make room for

My glory. Through each of these days I have been longing to pour out My glory, but each time I am ready, someone interrupts with another message, song or announcement. Every moment has been packed with programming."

A CALL TO DO NOTHING

Before I could ask God what all this meant for my final plenary session, He asked, "Would you make room for My glory during your last session in the morning? Are you willing to go to the lectern and do absolutely nothing? Will you stand there and simply trust Me to reveal My glory?"

I was stunned. What did He mean by "do absolutely nothing"? And what about my final integral lesson on becoming a prayer mobilizer? I had distributed three sets of worksheets. The third was still blank. The students would be awaiting the climactic message, so I thought.

Forgetting God's omniscience and foreknowledge, I said, "God, did You forget that my final session is the third of a three-part series? If I skip it, everyone will notice!"

Before I could say more, God asked again, "Will you make room for My glory?" He added, "All through this conference I've been looking for someone in leadership who would set aside their plans to make room for My glory.

Would you make room for My glory?"

It was now past 3 A.M., and although I was still uncertain as to what to do later that morning, I responded through tears, "Lord, whatever it takes, if You'll just give me courage, I will make room for Your glory."

LIQUID PRAYER

Before sunrise I quietly stepped into the shower; then I waited for my wife to awaken. I was dressed and sitting on the sofa when Dee finally showered and dressed. I asked her to sit beside me. I could not hold back the tears.

"Honey, what's wrong?" she asked.

"I didn't sleep at all last night," I answered. "God asked me to do something in my final session, and I'm not sure how to do it."

Confused, Dee asked, "What has He asked you to do?"

"Nothing!" I answered.

"What do you mean, 'nothing'?" she asked.

"That's it—*nothing!*" I responded.

Perplexed, Dee asked, "How do you just do nothing?"

It sounded silly, but I replied, "I have no idea. I've never just done 'nothing' before."

"But you can't just do nothing," Dee insisted.

"I know! But that's what God said. He wants me to set aside my third lesson and just go to the pulpit and wait for His glory."

My wife tried to pray for me, but each time she began to speak, she would weep. Suddenly, Dee was sobbing. I began my own petitioning. As I did, I felt God speak a final time. He said, "I have heard all of Dee's tears today."

As we left for the auditorium I remembered Charles Spurgeon's unique definition of a believer's tears. Spurgeon labeled them "liquid prayer"![1]

A RIVER OF INTIMACY

Stepping to the lectern I was both anxious and uncertain. *Here goes nothing,* I mused. My attempts at obedience that morning were further compounded by my introduction.

The emcee stressed how vital my final lesson would be. He proceeded to "fire up" the students, even sending ushers out into the aisles with extra worksheets in case some had forgotten theirs. I wanted to crawl into that proverbial hole to hide.

Thankfully, as I walked to the lectern, God gave me a simple directive. At least God's *nothing* would have a degree of direction. I was to ask students to turn to Isaiah 6 and get on their knees facing forward. Then I was to ask all of them to pray verses 1 through 8 aloud, not in unison but aloud at their own pace. God wanted all present to identify with Isaiah's vision of his encounter with God Himself.

The *nothing* part of my assignment would follow. Indeed, nothing else would be required because God was clearly in charge. What happened in the next 20 minutes none present could forget. Students with Bibles in hand were kneeling face forward, as a cacophony of voices filled the convention center. Within moments, I understood what God had intended to do.

Suddenly, without prompting, students began streaming into the aisles—getting on their faces. Brokenness spread across the auditorium.

Finally, my assigned hour was almost over. I turned to ask the emcee what to do, but he was prostrate under the piano, weeping. The worship team members were likewise scattered across the stage, each prostrate in prayer. Every delegate—all 5,000—was facedown before God. I had never seen anything like it.

The river of God's presence was clearly flowing. It was, uniquely, a river of both travail and delight. But more than that, it was a *river of intimacy*. And I knew that something was being born in those moments. The delight came with the same intensity that usually follows childbirth. The promise of the day before had come true, quite literally. The entire auditorium had become a womb of God's presence. Room had been made for God's glory, and when that crack in the door appeared, God's fullness flowed. Many students remained on their faces well into the afternoon.

> Room had been made for God's glory, and when that crack in the door appeared, God's fullness flowed.

By day's end extraordinary joy came. God had simply longed for these students to draw closer to Him, to allow the interruption of their plans and programs to seek Him alone. This experience showed me that all of His rivers of delight seem to begin with this *river of intimacy*. And it is in this river that we come to understand *the prophetic dimension of intercessory worship*.

BLESSINGS AND BIRTHINGS

It was, indeed, an extraordinary day. Our *nothing* had become

God's *something*—and it was a big something! That Texas convention center in December 1982 had truly become a womb of God's blessings and birthings! And it would become clear in later years that a river of God's presence had begun flowing—from that place that day—out to the nations.

Eight years later the leader who had been on his face under the piano at the convention, Bob Weiner, had a vision of a coming harvest of souls in the Soviet Union. It was December 1990, just a year before the Soviet Union would dissolve as a nation on Christmas Day 1991.

Starting with about 20 Russian Christians in February of that year, Bob Weiner had sent these believers out two by two to 300 major Russian cities and universities. Each team had one assignment: To identify one key believer with leadership potential in each of these cities and bring that person to Moscow for in-depth training.[2]

Just six weeks later, 300 new leaders arrived for the five days of in-depth training. After training, the leaders returned to their cities with one assignment: to win 10 other people to Christ. What followed in June was the conversion of 2,000 people who had come to Christ through Bob Weiner's initial group that went to Moscow. After similar training, the 2,000 new believers were also sent out. From 1991 to 1996, Bob trained 16,000 potential leaders! During that time more than 250 churches were planted, some of which now have more than 1,500 members. I believe that river of God's presence released at the Texas convention center over a decade earlier flowed all the way to Russia.

I, too, was caught up in that Texas river. In January 1991, I made my first trip to Russia with our newly appointed Russian coordinator for Every Home for Christ, Paul Ilyin. We laid the groundwork for a plan to reach every home in all 15 Soviet Republics. By January 2001, just 10 years later, more than 36 million households had been personally visited and reached with the gospel. Hundreds of thousands of letters and decision cards had been followed up with Bible lessons, and several hundred churches had been planted. One of those churches, in the Ukraine, has more than 4,500 believers. More recently, Operation Siberia was launched to reach every city, town and remote village in this vast desolate region, home by home.

When I experienced the flow of that Texas river in 1982, I was not involved with the ministry of Every Home for Christ. I had no idea that just a few years later I would be leading this ministry, which is reaching over 20 million new families in more than 100 nations annually with the gospel.

HEAVEN'S HARVEST SONG

It was not until 12 years after the Texas convention that I began to understand the prophetic nature of those moments in Texas and its relationship to a "last-days" movement of worship and intercession (which some refer to as "intercessory worship"). I became convinced that God would release rivers of His delight into the nations through this movement.

Two passages of Scripture highlighting intercessory worship (introduced as the Harp and Bowl Movement in my previous two books, *Heights of Delight* and *Pathways of Delight*) are (1) the apostle James's reference to an end-times restoration of the Tabernacle of David, no doubt depicting a global movement of extravagant worship as in David's day (see Acts 15:16-18); and (2) the account in Revelation 5:8-10 that shows heavenly beings coming before God's throne holding harps (symbols of worship) and bowls (containing prayers of the saints) that release a new song. It is heaven's song of an end-times harvest picturing multitudes being redeemed "from every tribe and language and people and nation" (Rev. 5:9).

These references are profoundly significant to the release of God's rivers of the prophetic gifts in our generation. I believe intercessory worship is key to this release. It links the harp and bowl symbols creating in its worship-saturated intercession. The term "intercessory worship" refers to concentrated worship that becomes intercessory in nature because it carries the prayers of God's people before God's throne as incense. As a result, God releases His power to accomplish His purposes for the harvest (see Rev. 5:8-10; 8:1-6).

Because of the nature of such God-saturated worship, it often becomes uniquely prophetic, a theme we will depict in subsequent chapters as different rivers from God. But first, what do we mean by "prophetic worship"?

THE WINDS OF WORSHIP

A study of prophetic "intercessory worship" must begin with a look at the word "prophecy" itself.

Both the Greek and Hebrew words for "prophecy" in the Bible mean "to speak before" or "to speak in front of."[3] In John's Revelation we find a phrase referring to Christ and the subject of prophecy: "For the testimony of

Jesus is the spirit of prophecy" (Rev. 19:10). Jack Hayford explains this subject in the *Spirit Filled Life Bible*.

> The entire Bible is a product of the Holy Spirit, who is not only "the Spirit of truth" (John 16:13), but also "the Spirit of prophecy" (Revelation 19:10). The verb "to prophesy" (derived from the Greek preposition *pro* and verb *pehmi*) means "to speak from before." The preposition "before" in this use may mean: (1) "in advance" and/or (2) "in front of." Thus *to prophesy* is a proper term to describe the proclamation of God's Word as it forecasts events. It may also describe the declaration of God's Word forthrightly, boldly, or confrontingly before a group of individuals—telling forth God's truth and will. So, in both respects, the Bible is prophetic: A Book that reveals God's will through His Word and His words, as well as a Book that reveals God's plan and predictions.[4]

When we speak of prophetic worship, we are speaking of prophecy but as it is applied to our worship. Worship, in this sense, might be used by God to declare what may happen in the future or to simply deliver a message from His heart.

Interestingly, a message from God delivered through prophetic praise or worship might actually be delivered into the heavenlies *before* "principalities" and "rulers of the darkness" (Eph. 6:12, *NKJV*) to announce God's intended will. Such worship thus becomes an act of spiritual warfare, even as the worshipers are exalting God. It becomes intercessory when the worship releases God's power into the circumstances of others, usually by first binding or restraining the invisible, dark powers.

PRAISING PROPHETICALLY

It is clear that in David's day prophetic praise or worship was clearly understood. Of this reality, Jack Hayford writes:

> After raising the tabernacle in Jerusalem and anticipating the building of the temple, David organized and provided for the support of music leaders and ministries to enhance Israel's worship (see 1 Chronicles 25:2-7). Choirs and orchestras not only prepared to sing and play skillfully, but they also were selected for their sensitivity to the spirit of prophecy.[5]

Notice the worship team David established around the Tabernacle: "David and the army commanders then appointed men from the families of Asaph, Heman, and Jeduthun to proclaim God's messages to the accompaniment of harps, lyres, and cymbals" (1 Chron. 25:1, *NLT*). To "proclaim God's messages" with musical accompaniment refers to prophetic worship.

Later in the passage we are given the names of six worship leaders "who prophesied, using the harp in thanking and praising the LORD" (1 Chron. 25:3). Then in verse 7, we are told that 288 other worshipers were similarly involved, and all were "trained and skilled in music for the LORD."

Therefore, these worshipers were not only skilled, but they were taught prophetic worship. Jack Hayford further adds:

This description reveals a blend of both spontaneity to the Holy Spirit and preparedness for skilled musical presentation. Their prophesying involved more than setting existing Scripture to music. These musicians were to wait on the Lord for inspiration—living truth that would ignite worship and joy in the hearts of God's people.[6]

Suggesting that we need this same ministry in the Church today, Hayford queries:

> Moses longed for the day that all of God's people would prophesy (see Numbers 11:29); shouldn't we also expect our choirs and instruments to minister with the gift of prophecy? Isn't it possible that the New Testament restoration of the Tabernacle of David may bring to us new dimensions of Holy Spirit-inspired praise and worship in song?[7]

I believe the answers to Hayford's questions are a resounding yes and that prophesying is beginning to happen in the global harp and bowl intercessory worship movement. This movement, I am convinced, will help release rivers of God's presence that will transform and heal entire nations through the gospel of Christ.

The psalmist sees this link between prophetic worship and the harvest. He sang:

> All you have made will praise you, O LORD; your saints will extol you. They will tell of the glory of your kingdom and speak of your might, so that all

men may know of your mighty acts and the glorious splendor of your kingdom (Ps. 145:10-12).

DEEP AND WIDE: A WORD ABOUT RIVERS

All of this, I believe, will culminate as a glorious prophetic river of God's presence in all its fullness, to be released through our worship and channeled by our intercession. The psalmist pictured this river when he wrote, "There is a river whose streams make glad the city of God, the holy place where the Most High dwells. God is within her, she will not fall; God will help her at break of day" (Ps. 46:4-5).

> To get into the river is to get into God, and that is intimacy!

The psalmist pictures a river with various streams that flow from God's dwelling place. God Himself is in the midst of the city and thus the river. Some would contend the river *is* God—the flow of His very presence by His Spirit—which is why I define our first river in this study as a *river of intimacy*. To get into the river is to get into God, and that is intimacy!

Ezekiel likewise described a life-giving river and saw in it God's healing power in Ezekiel 47:1-12. When the prophet first steps in, the river's depth suddenly increases. It reaches the prophet's ankles and then it rises to his knees. Next, the river's at his waist. Soon Ezekiel testifies, "The river was too deep to cross without swimming" (v. 5, NLT). The prophet continues, "Suddenly, to my surprise, many trees were now growing on both sides of the river!" (v. 7, NLT).

The prophet is envisioning a picture of life and health. He explains, "Everything that touches the water of this river will live. . . . Wherever this water flows, everything will live" (v. 9, NLT).

Generations later the apostle John would receive his revelation and describe what scholars contend was the same river Ezekiel described. John would write:

Then the angel showed me the river of the water of life, as clear as crystal, flowing from the throne of God and of the Lamb down the middle of the great street of the city. On each side of the river stood the tree of life, bearing twelve crops of fruit, yielding its fruit every month. And the leaves of the tree are for the healing of the nations (Rev. 22:1-2).

If the river that flows from the throne of God is His very presence, then to step into it is to step into a *river of intimacy* with the Father. The deeper we swim in that river, the greater the intimacy.

In recent years much has been spoken and written about authority in spiritual warfare. But as Alice Smith wisely says, "Your authority in warfare will never exceed your intimacy in worship."[8]

The *river of intimacy* is the fountainhead where all the other rivers of delight begin. And to stay in its flow, one needs to respond daily to God's admonition—"Make room for My glory."

A CONCH-SHELL ENCOUNTER

RIVER OF SUFFICIENCY: THE POSITIONAL DIMENSION OF INTERCESSORY WORSHIP

Tibet sits atop the world—a high place in more ways than one. In recent months a trickle of a river of God's healing presence has begun flowing across this historic Buddhist land. It all began with a prophetic worship encounter at a sacred conch shell in Lhasa, Tibet.

The conch-shell encounter happened to a friend, Mark Geppert, and a team of worshiping intercessors who went with him to Tibet in August 1998. There, at the famed Jokhang Temple, the confrontation occurred.

Mark's unique experience introduces us to the *positional dimension of prophetic intercessory worship*. Simply stated, intercessory worship has the capacity to position God's people in a special place of prophetic authority. When that authority is exercised, something of the satanic influence of a city, region or entire nation begins to diminish. And that is what I believe is happening in Tibet, the birthplace of the Dalai Lama and Tibetan Buddhism.

A CHINESE BIRD DOG

Mark took his team to Tibet to pray at the Potala Palace (the home of the Dalai Lama, who actually resides in exile in Dharamsala, India) and at the Jokhang Temple, the center of all of Tibetan Buddhism. They also hoped to distribute a large quantity of evangelistic literature, as they had on past journeys.

Mark and his team had developed a unique prayer strategy during previous visits to Tibet (and elsewhere in Asia). Several years earlier Mark had met a Chinese brother,

Hubert Chan, in Singapore, and together the two had developed this unusual way of working—especially in difficult places like Tibet. Mark would serve as a foreign distraction, while Hubert became, in Mark's words, "a Chinese bird dog."

This is how they worked: Because Mark is a white foreigner, the locals would closely watch him. Hubert, on the other hand, being Chinese, blends into the cultures of Asia. So, while Mark would wait outside a place like the Jokhang Temple, actually *hoping* to be noticed, Hubert would go inside and, as Mark explained, seek out the "strongman" of that particular place. Mark describes a "strongman" as a person who, through spiritual influences, controls or affects the population of a geographical region or seems to have unusual authority over an area. Mark's team learned to spiritually discern who these individuals were.

Their strategy involves praying in person for that leader whenever possible (obviously with the person's permission) and even anointing him or her with oil. According to Mark, it has been amazing how often they have been granted such permission.

Mark is convinced that by taking a strongman's hands and praying, some sort of flow of the Holy Spirit begins. And although the strongman is not aware of all that is happening, Mark feels this prayer has the capacity to restrain demonic activity in the strongman, potentially breaking the power by which he or she influences that area. According to Mark, this is something they have seen happen with unusual success in numerous places throughout Asia. Already they have prayed in this way for a governor, a mayor, several monks, mediums, military leaders and even a sultan. All welcomed their prayers and even permitted Mark or one of his team members to anoint them with oil. Interestingly, in several cases following such encounters, there has been a noticeable increase in openness to hearing the gospel in the immediate area. Mark is sure this strategy has helped make a difference.

ENTERTAINING THE TROOPS

With this strategy in mind, Mark and Hubert and their team arrived outside Lhasa's Jokhang Temple on a mild summer day in August 1998. As usual, Mark "entertained the troops" (drawing attention from police authorities), while Hubert slipped into the temple to find the senior abbot. This would be the man second in command to the exiled Dalai Lama.

Hubert found the abbot and told him their group had heard he was ill, which they had, and that a "fat holy man from the West" had come to bless him. The fat holy man, of course, was Mark Geppert, who readily admits he fits at least the first part of that description. The abbot was moved by Hubert's words and quickly invited the team in.

It was a most significant moment. Almost immediately the abbot agreed to receive the group between the conch shell—a venerated artifact embedded in the floor of the Jokhang Temple—and the Jowo Sakyamuni Buddha, the oldest and most revered Buddha statue in Tibet. The latter was brought there from China around A.D. 639 by King Songsten Gampo's Chinese wife, Princess Wencheng.

Regarding the conch shell, Mark explained that Buddhist devotees come from across Tibet and around the world to kneel before it. Many bow so that their foreheads touch the shell. Mark explained, "I've seen some Buddhist worshipers shake violently and their eyes actually roll into their heads while bowing before the shell. It's frightening."

The conch shell's significance in the Jokhang Temple, as Mark told me, came from another ancient legend, of which there are many. According to this one, Princess Wencheng had thrown this very shell into what was then Lhasa's Lake Wothang and, suddenly, land rose up. She thus determined to build a temple for her treasured Buddha where the land had risen up.

In reference to the Jowo Sakyamuni Buddha, there is little doubt of the significance of this statue to Tibetan Buddhists. Depicting Buddha as a 12-year-old, this relic is believed to represent the beginnings of firmly established Buddhism in Tibet. Until that time the religion had been rejected in Tibet, even though all other countries of the region had long embraced the teachings of Buddha. But Tibet soon became the world's great Buddhist stronghold. Indeed, not long after Princess Wencheng brought the image of Jowo Sakyamuni to Tibet, King Gampo went so far as to pass a law making it illegal *not* to be a Buddhist in Tibet.[1]

Somehow this statue was (and is!) a stronghold in and of itself. From its arrival in the seventh century, it has brought the very throne of global Buddhism to Tibet. And here, before this famed Sakyamuni Buddha, just a few steps from the sacred conch shell, Mark's team would engage in prophetic intercessory worship.

ANOINTING THE ABBOT

There is a 10-foot space between the embedded conch shell and the Buddha. Both are housed deep within the

Jokhang Temple. It was into that space that the abbot invited Mark's team. Through an interpreter, Mark asked if the abbot would permit them to anoint him with oil. The abbot agreed.

Mark then anointed the elderly Buddhist with oil and prayed. He recalls the exact words that began his prayer, "We take authority over all that pertains to you in the name of Jesus!" After adding a further blessing, asking God to touch the abbot's body, Mark gave him literature about Jesus in the Tibetan language. This probably was the first occasion the man was ever given a clear opportunity to know about Jesus.

The abbot was so touched by this act that he unlocked the large, 15-foot-wide chain grail (gate) covering the entry before the Buddha. He then ushered the entire team into the presence of Tibetan Buddhism's greatest treasure—the Jowo Sakyamuni Buddha.

Mark has no idea how many millions of people worldwide either worship directly or are influenced by demonic forces connected to this Buddha and conch shell. He believes these forces directly impact New Age and Tibetan Buddhism influences worldwide. And amazingly, Mark's team was given entry by the senior abbot of the Jokhang Temple to stand in this very place to exalt Christ.

BUILDING A THRONE

According to Mark, the walkway around the 5-foot-high Buddha was just wide enough for their team of 20 to make a complete circle. The abbot departed, leaving them alone in the small chapel for 30 minutes. The team of worshipers surrounded the Buddha and sang the "blood medley," including old hymns such as "There Is Power in the Blood" and "Oh, the Blood of Jesus." More as a prophetic directive than a song, they also sang Paul Kyle's inspiring chorus:

> Jesus, we enthrone You,
> We proclaim You are King.
> Standing here in the midst of us,
> We raise You up with our praise.
> And as we worship, build a throne;
> And as we worship, build a throne;
> And as we worship, build a throne;
> Come Lord Jesus and take Your place.[2]

As the team sang, they sensed a supernatural enthroning of God's presence within the chamber. They felt that what they were singing was actually happening. Although careful not to draw too much attention to themselves, the group still worshiped openly. This was, no doubt, highly unusual for the Jokhang Temple. Still, the abbot did not interrupt. The team concluded by anointing the Sakyamuni Buddha itself with oil, even as they continued worshiping. Mark said it was dripping with oil. Though no one in the group understood all that was happening, it was clearly an act of prophetic intercessory worship.

They left the Jokhang Temple, and in less than 30 minutes they distributed at least 2,000 messages about Jesus in the Tibetan language. Mark first asked a policeman if this would be permissible. Once the officer was assured the literature did not mention the Dalai Lama (and especially did not contain his picture) they were allowed to freely distribute the literature. The policeman even offered to help hand out the booklets. (Chinese authorities that control Tibet consider the Dalai Lama a significant political threat. Even his picture is treated as contraband and is thus illegal.) Mark and the team were certain the impact of their intercessory worship moments earlier, and their strategy of anointing a strongman, the abbot, was already taking effect.

But that was only the beginning of this trickle of God's river of healing that began flowing that pleasant

August day. Very soon the trickle would become a stream of God's blessing.

THE LANGUAGE OF TEARS

Two months later Mark returned to Lhasa with yet another team. In addition to other sites, the team went to Tibet's famed Sera Monastery, one of the two significant Gelugpa monasteries in Lhasa. The Gelugpa order of Tibetan Buddhism is the main Buddhist order in Tibet associated with the Dalai Lama. (As other religions, Christianity and Islam included, Buddhism has its branches or denominations.)

While the rest of the team went in different directions, Mark sat alone on a wooden bench, quietly worshiping Jesus in front of a large stone Buddha. Such quiet praying was not out of place in the Tibetan culture in which meditation and reflection are the norm. Sitting near Mark was a monk reading his prayers. The monk was holding a tile inscribed with ancient Buddhist prayers written in Sanskrit. Mark began praying quietly for the monk, asking God for an open door to share Christ with him. Mark's biggest challenge was the language barrier. He did not speak Tibetan, and he was sure the monk did not speak English.

Mark had an idea. He took a gospel message in Tibetan from his pocket and held it in front of him in the same manner the monk was holding his tile. Of course, Mark could not read a word of the tract, but he knew its message. It told how God had only one Son, Jesus, who came to live among men to sacrifice His life so that all who believed might have eternal life. It is a message totally foreign to a Tibetan Buddhist.

Mark's strategy paid off. Out of the corner of his eye, he could see the Buddhist worshiper gazing intently at his booklet. The monk was interested because he could see it was in his language; and, as Mark explained, most Tibetan readers believe that anything written in their "high language" must be a message from God.

Noting the monk's interest, Mark offered him the booklet. Amazingly, the monk promptly replaced the tile with the tract and began reading it as prayerfully as he had been reading the tile. Suddenly the monk closed the tract and began weeping. Mark sensed what was happening. He realized the man had just read the part about praying the sinner's prayer. He was certain the monk had just prayed that prayer.

Now Mark was weeping too. He put his arms around the monk who put his face on Mark's shoulder. It was an unusual scene. For several minutes the two shared in the language of tears.

GROUNDWORK FOR A MIRACLE

The river of God's presence was, undoubtedly, beginning to flow. But it was about to be released in ways Mark could never have imagined. Those moments with the monk had been observed closely by a Chinese authority standing unobserved in the shadows. He had watched the white foreigner praying and had seen the monk meditating. He had noticed the exchange of the tract and the highly unusual display of emotions. Tibetans simply do not hug each other in public, let alone in tearful sobs.

As Mark regained his composure, he looked up to see a tall, well-dressed Chinese man approaching. He was not a Tibetan but a Han Chinese man. Mark's heart raced. He was sure he had been caught red-handed. He had experienced this feeling in China before—three times, in fact. Each time it had happened because authorities had caught him witnessing for Jesus. All three times he had been deported immediately. Mark braced himself for number four.

However, God had something else in mind. The intercessory worship team that anointed the abbot and the

Buddha statue two months earlier had laid the groundwork for a miracle.

"Thank you for caring for that monk," the tall Chinese man said in English.

His gentleness surprised Mark. He had expected a rebuke but was given a compliment.

Catching his breath, Mark responded, "Not at all," uncertain what to say next.

"May I know who you are?" the Chinese man asked in a friendly voice.

"Please do not be offended," Mark answered. He then continued, "But first, may I know who you are?"

Mark had learned discretion in times like these. Do not say too much until you know who is asking the questions and why.

The man presented his business card, which revealed that he was the public health director for all of Tibet. The man represented the government of China in Beijing.

Mark introduced himself as leading a small foundation in the United States, not explaining that his foundation's primary focus was prayer.

Mark was surprised by the next question.

"Would your foundation be interested in a health project for Tibet?"

By now, several of Mark's team members had gathered and were listening in. "Yes, we would," Mark responded on behalf of the group.

The health director asked, "What type of health project would you like to do in Tibet?"

Mark had no idea what to suggest, so he simply responded, "You are the director. Why don't you recommend a project, and we'll see if we can help?"

Mark was hoping it would involve something at least within the realm of possibility for his small ministry or perhaps one that God could use to help his group serve as a catalyst for others. They agreed to meet again that evening at the team's hotel to discuss a specific project.

A RIVER OF SUFFICIENCY

The meeting was held that night as planned. The health director came with his representatives from the People's Regional Hospital of Tibet. In the brief hours between Mark's encounter with the health director and the evening meeting, the health director's team members had already formulated an idea they wanted to propose. They suggested Mark's group consider joining them in a partnership to help identify and meet the needs of children with heart defects in Tibet. The project would be called

The Survey and Treatment of Congenital Heart Disease Among Children in the Autonomous Region of Tibet.

The sweeping objective would include examining all school-aged children of Tibet, beginning in the Lhasa area, to determine the extent of congenital heart disease among Tibetan adolescents. (Apparently a major side effect of Tibet's unusually high altitude is damage to the hearts of young children.) The project would include providing education for health professionals, obtaining necessary equipment for the task and, ultimately, helping raise funds needed for corrective surgery for those who could not afford it (which would probably mean all who needed the surgery!).

Mark's foundation also was asked to participate in the general upgrading of the main hospital in Lhasa to help with the project. It was a huge assignment, but Mark reminded himself that we have a big God! Mark was about to learn that one of God's rivers of delight is a *river of sufficiency.*

BLESS THEIR HEARTS!

Late that night, together with several Chinese leaders, Mark initialed the protocol for the project. Although the launching would be delayed for another year due to the bombing of the Chinese Embassy in Belgrade, Yugoslavia (during the war in the Balkans), the following year everything was approved. On January 26, 2000, Mark signed the final agreement. By July 17, 2000, several trained medical teams saw their first young patients.

To date, Mark's teams have examined 7,000 children. Soon 10,000 children a year will be examined. Thus far, four percent have abnormalities that require medical attention. As is typical with Mark, he developed a way in the examination process for their medical "intercessors" to lay hands on every child and consecrate each child to Jesus! Each child is then told the story of Jesus. "It's a way to bless their hearts in more ways than one," Mark says.

Obviously, there has been much warfare surrounding this project. Yet many intercessors have become involved in praying for this unique transformation strategy that could ultimately release God's river of healing to all of the children of Tibet—both spiritually and physically.

Mark also desires to establish a 24-hour prayer covering to confront all the difficulties head-on. These obstacles include the financial challenge. The 5-million-dollar budget over a four-year period would seem daunting for a ministry operating on less than $100,000 annually. But Mark's faith is growing. Recently a hospital in Pittsburgh donated a heart catheterization lab for the project. Its value is $2 million. That same week a respected humanitarian ministry agreed to help raise $3 million for refurbishing a cardio-surgical unit in a large wing at Tibet's major hospital. The wing will be key in caring for children from across Tibet with heart defects. God's *river of sufficiency* was definitely flowing. Mark figures he is at least up to his ankles!

A SUPERNATURAL REALITY

There's something uniquely symbolic in what is happening in Tibet, especially when it comes to the release of rivers. What is a geological reality in the physical realm could become a supernatural reality in the spiritual realm. Geologically, Tibet lies on a vast plateau as large as Western Europe, sandwiched between two Himalayan ridges five miles high. Geologists tell us this plateau is the source of all the major rivers in South and East Asia including the Indus, Sutleg and Brahmaputra from the far western highlands of Tibet and the Mekong, Salween, Yangzi, Gyron, Yellow, Minjiang, and Jialing from Tibet's eastern region.[3] All of these rivers flowing *below* begin from *above* in Tibet.

Supernaturally speaking, Tibet also has been the primary source of the flow of both Tibetan Buddhism as well as New Age occultism and mysticism throughout the world. The Dalai Lama, for example, is one of the world's most worshiped and revered living figures of our time. His influence is directly tied to Tibet.

Could it be that intercessory worship is beginning to change all this, starting at the very "roof of the world"—Tibet? Rivers that flow from Tibet clearly stream downward, impacting all that is below. This appears to be true both physically and spiritually. I believe a river of God's presence has begun flowing across Tibet, and it, too, will soon flow downward. It could very well impact all that is within its path.

I am not sure how many statues of Buddha in the world have been anointed with oil and bathed in the sounds of Christian intercessory worship, but I know of at least one—and it is at the top of the world. I believe that this unusual anointing has opened a stream of God's presence that will flow out to all the world.

THE POWER OF PROPHETIC POSITIONING

Mark's conch-shell encounter at Tibet's sacred Sukyamuni Buddha illustrates what I believe is *the positional dimension of prophetic intercessory worship*. Such worship, and its resulting intercession, leads us into the *river of God's sufficiency* just as it did Jehoshaphat and God's people in ancient Israel, as revealed in 2 Chronicles 20:1-26. Facing a formidable coalition army of Moabites, Ammonites and Meunites, Jehoshaphat almost seems to have given up before the battle begins. Then, as war appears imminent, he calls the nation to prayer.

God responds with a prophetic word. His Spirit comes upon Jahaziel, who proclaims, "This is what the LORD says: Do not be afraid! Don't be discouraged by this mighty army, for the battle is not yours, but God's" (v. 15, NLT). The prophet adds, "You will not even need to fight. Take your positions; then stand still and watch the LORD's victory" (v. 17, NLT).

It is clear from this familiar passage that the response of God's people and their king was to position themselves in praise. We read, "Then King Jehoshaphat bowed down with his face to the ground. And all the people of Judah and Jerusalem did the same, worshiping the LORD" (v. 18, NLT).

Most students of Scripture recall the outcome of this battle and how prophetic worship was involved. We read, "After consulting the leaders of the people, the king appointed singers to walk ahead of the army, singing to the LORD and praising him for his holy splendor" (v. 21,

NLT). Note the immediate result, *"At the moment they began to sing and give praise*, the LORD caused the armies of Ammon, Moab, and Mount Seir to start fighting among themselves" (v. 22, *NLT*, emphasis added).

God's intervention literally caused these armies to defeat themselves. And it happened instantly. But there was more. Through this victory came a remarkable release of resources. God's *river of sufficiency* was flowing. Scripture says, "King Jehoshaphat and his men went out to gather the plunder. They found vast amounts of equipment, clothing, and other valuables—more than they could carry" (v. 25, *NLT*).

> As intercession, worship calls upon and releases onto the battlefield God's power to intervene.

Such is the power of prophetic positioning—and intercessory worship is clearly a key. Note again the phrase in the text, "At the moment they began to sing and give praise, the Lord caused the armies . . . to start fighting among themselves" (v. 22, *NLT*).

Here we see how worship, itself, becomes *intercessory*. As intercession, it calls upon and releases onto the battlefield God's power to intervene. The position was also obviously one of *worship*. It was likewise *prophetic*, because God's people were making their declarations of worship "before" or "in front of" the opposing armies. (As you will recall from the last chapter, this fits our definition of prophecy.) Even more, they were declaring their worship *into the heavenlies*, summoning God's intervention, which also is intercessory. Thus we have a clear picture of *prophetic intercessory worship*.

What Mark Geppert's team did in Tibet was not unlike what Jehoshaphat's army did in ancient Judah. They moved into position, and that position was prophetic intercessory worship.

Today a river of God's sufficiency has begun flowing throughout Tibet, and it seems ready to break forth into the valleys below. Fortunately this river is not reserved for only a few bold warriors who happen to travel to faraway places like Tibet to pray. This river of God's delight, one of several we will examine on these pages, flows anywhere His people are willing to wait long enough in worship to freely drink. Shall we gather at the river?

AGATHA'S INTERCESSORS

RIVER OF SUPREMACY: THE PENETRATING DIMENSION OF INTERCESSORY WORSHIP

It was a sunny morning as the phone rang in our hotel room. There was little indication a severe storm was heading our way as I looked out across beautiful Hong Kong Harbor. It was Sunday, September 26, 1999. I was to speak at two services that morning and then conclude a three-day conference on spiritual warfare that afternoon.

Over 100 churches had sent delegates to the previous sessions.

The conference theme, Light the Window, had a particular emphasis on preparing intercessors for a month-long prayer focus for the 10/40 Window, slated for the following month, October. The 10/40 Window is a term that was popularized in the 1990s through the AD2000 and Beyond Movement directed by Luis Bush, the originator of the term, "10/40 Window."

This region is marked by the boundaries of 10 degrees north of the equator to 40 degrees north and stretches from the west coast of Africa to the eastern border of China. The region is home to 97 percent of the world's least-evangelized nations. Yet it only has 8 percent of the world's missionary force laboring there. The 10/40 Window is also the headquarters of most of the world's largest non-Christian religions: Islam, Hinduism and Buddhism.

PRAYING THROUGH THE WINDOW

Every Home for Christ, the ministry I direct, had been deeply involved in mobilizing prayer for this region since the term "10/40 Window" first became familiar. It was at our EHC Colorado Springs headquarters on June 12, 1992, that a handful of leaders met at the request of Luis Bush to discuss the feasibility of having an entire month of world-wide focused prayer concentrated on this region. Few realized as we met that morning that the largest focused prayer movement for the nations was being born during those few hours.

We met in our ministry's boardroom, adjacent to our prayer room, which was filled with intercessors from local churches. They had been invited to prayerfully "cover" what we believed was to be a strategic meeting. By noon the theme, Pray Through the Window, had emerged, and an ambitious goal had been set of mobilizing 1 million Christians globally to pray for these 10/40 Window nations (two nations per day) during October 1993, the following year. In that way, synchronized, focused prayer would touch all 62 nations during the 31 days of October. An idea also was born to send teams of intercessors into each of those 62 countries.

I had my doubts that 62 teams could be mobilized for such a task, and I was skeptical that 1 million people could be enlisted to pray for this region for an entire month.

But to my delight, when all the groups, denominations, local churches and ministries reported their numbers, over 20 million had participated and an amazing 249 prayer journeys were taken. The committee decided to sponsor a similar monthlong focus every other year through the end of the decade.

October 1999, following our conference in Hong Kong, was to be the final monthlong prayer focus of the decade for the 10/40 Window. For this final thrust an even more ambitious goal had been set: mobilizing 50 million intercessors to pray for this region at least five minutes daily throughout the month. Because several million of these intercessors would be mobilized by radio across China's mainland (as well as among China's vast network of house churches) it seemed appropriate to have a special 10/40 Window focus meeting in Hong Kong.

The auditorium, which seated 800, had been filled for the first two days of sessions, with scores of interested intercessors turned away due to lack of space. It was clear that believers in Hong Kong recognized the significance of the hour and the need to focus prayer on China's mainland as well as other nearby nations of the 10/40 Window.

ANTICIPATING CAM!

So as the phone rang that Sunday morning in Hong Kong, I was looking forward to the final session of the conference that afternoon. A day earlier we had announced that this last session would be a special time for an intercessors' impartation, a time of laying on of hands for those interested, praying that God would impart to them a special anointing for more effective intercession. I particularly promised to pray specifically for those who wanted to be involved in concentrated prayer the following month. My hope was that numerous teams of intercessors from Hong Kong would journey to the mainland for prayer during the next month, joining others who would be coming from around the world to the 10/40 Window. Our committee had set a goal of 3,000 prayer journeys throughout the region, including mainland China. For this reason I felt that the final session was especially critical.

The phone call appeared to change all that. It was Agatha, the conference coordinator. Tropical Storm Cam, that we had heard about several days earlier when it was far south and heading toward Taiwan, had changed directions and was now moving directly toward Hong Kong. It was rapidly becoming a full-blown typhoon, already reaching a Signal 8, only two degrees below the highest possible level for typhoons in the region. Agatha explained that when a warning reached a Signal 8, all public transportation had to be shut down and public facilities closed. This meant there would be no church services that morning and the final session of the conference would need to be canceled.

But Agatha was not about to give up. True, a Signal 8 storm was heading our way, and no storm of this magnitude had ever changed directions again when so close, but Agatha decided to bring together a small group of intercessors to pray anyway.

We had known for several days the possibility of bad weather that weekend. But because the typhoon had been heading toward Taiwan it caused us little concern. Now all that had changed. Cam was coming!

Interestingly, the storm's turn toward us may well have had something to do with the prayers of participants on the first day of our conference. A few weeks earlier Taiwan had suffered a devastating earthquake. So when intercessors in Hong Kong heard that Typhoon Cam was heading toward the area in Taiwan where massive relief efforts were under way, Agatha suggested they ask God to change the direction of the typhoon. And it happened. Apparently no one thought to pray that if it did change direction, it not head our way.

PRAYING STRATEGICALLY

Cam was closing in, and Hong Kong was closing down—except for Agatha's intercessors. Though there was no public transportation, a small team still showed up at Agatha's office by midmorning. The wind had picked up noticeably, and dark clouds gathered on the horizon. Hotel staff members had come to our room and affixed huge strips of tape on the windows facing Hong Kong Harbor. If the windows broke, the tape would help keep pieces from flying haphazardly. This was not terribly encouraging, so we headed down to the lobby.

Meanwhile, Agatha's team had assembled. Soon their worship and warfare had begun. The small group decided to pray through the seven steps for strategic prayer that I had taught the previous afternoon. I had taken the seven steps from my book *The Jericho Hour*. I had begun the session by defining strategic-level prayer, highlighting the fact that "strategic" suggests that which counts the most. Strategic-level prayer, I explained, is prayer at a level that really counts. It is prayer of truly eternal consequences.

For comparison, I suggested that there's a big difference in praying for a toothache as compared to praying for the salvation of an unreached people group. The latter is clearly more strategic (unless, of course, it's *your* toothache!).

I proceeded to list seven primary characteristics of strategic praying, including a key word to expand each aspect and a core attribute (or quality of spirit) high-lighted by a particular characteristic. The list included:

1. Authoritative Praying

First, I suggested that strategic-level prayer is *authoritative*, expanding the definition with the key word—"confident." Authoritative praying, I explained, embodies *a spirit of audacity*. Such praying believes and claims the promise of Jesus: "I have given you authority to trample on snakes and scorpions and to overcome all the power of the enemy; nothing will harm you" (Luke 10:19).

A meaningful pattern for such praying is found in God's promise to Jeremiah: "See, I have this day set thee over the nations and over the kingdoms, to root out, and to pull down, and to destroy, and to throw down, to build, and to plant" (Jer. 1:10, *KJV*). I suggested we can take these six specific assignments (i.e. root out, pull down, destroy, etc.) and turn them into audacious praying that leads to strategic results.

2. Combative Praying

Second, I emphasized that strategic-level prayer is *combative*. My key word for this point was—"aggressive." Combative praying is to pray with *a spirit of militancy*. I reminded participants that Scripture is filled with military symbol-ism. I cited Joshua 5:14-15; 2 Corinthians 10:4-5; Ephesians 6:10-18; 1 Timothy 6:12; and 2 Timothy 2:3-4. I explained that the very phrase "Lord of hosts," which appears 273 times in the Old Testament, means "heavenly army." Even in Exodus God is described as "a man of war" (Exod. 15:3, *KJV*). Combative praying, I suggested, is to put "fight" into our intercession.

3. Intensive Praying

Third, I emphasized that strategic-level prayer is *intensive*. This, I told the group, is summarized in the word "fer-vent." Such praying expresses *a spirit of determination*. James describes it as, "The effectual fervent prayer of a righteous man availeth much" (Jas. 5:16, *KJV*). *The Amplified Bible* translates this verse as, "The earnest (heartfelt, continued) prayer of a righteous man makes tremendous power avail-able [dynamic in its working]."

I noted that the English word "intense," meaning "existing in an extreme degree," comes from the Latin *intensus*, meaning "stretched tight."[1] There are occasions, I suggested, when "uptight" prayers are in order. Nehemiah was "uptight," or "stretched tight," when he wept for many days in prayer because of the conditions of God's people in exile and the fallen walls of Jerusalem (see Neh. 1:1-4). Christ was "stretched tight" when His sweat became as blood during His intense Gethsemane prayer encounter (see Luke 22:44). There is little doubt these prayer encounters were strategic!

4. Confrontational Praying

I next highlighted that strategic-level prayer is *confrontational*—suggesting the key word as "boldness." Confrontational praying, I explained, manifests itself in *a spirit of tenacity.* Perhaps this is what Jesus pictured when He told His disciples they could command mountains to be moved (see Mark 11:22-23). I added that a combination of the first three characteristics on the list—authoritative, combative and intensive prayer—all combine to produce the boldness needed for confrontational praying. Such praying becomes boldly tenacious or, as a colleague once personally described it, *praying with a passionate tenacity and a touch of insanity.*

5. Comprehensive Praying

Fifth, I suggested that strategic-level prayer is *comprehensive.* This is summarized in the key word "focused." If our intercession is to be comprehensive, it must have a clear focus.

Such praying, I added, requires *a spirit of totality*. This means we should fully address a particular issue in prayer—comprehensively. Jesus said, "And all things, whatsoever ye shall ask in prayer, believing, ye shall receive" (Matt. 21:22, KJV). The *New International Version* translates this verse as, "If you believe, you will receive whatever you ask for in prayer." "Whatsoever" or "whatever" is a sweeping expression that involves totality in our praying.

> If our intercession is to be comprehensive, it must have a clear focus, which means we should fully address a particular issue in prayer—comprehensively.

6. Creative Praying

Next, I defined strategic-level prayer as being *creative*, emphasizing the key word as "faith." This kind of praying, I suggested, involves *a spirit of vision*. It is to allow God to use our imaginations to help us pray creatively. Creative praying stretches our faith. Paul said: God "quickeneth the dead, and calleth those things which be not as though they were" (Rom. 4:17, *KJV*). The author of Hebrews explains: "Now faith is being sure of what we hope for and certain of what we do not see" (Heb. 11:1). Such faith, someone suggested, is to reach into nowhere, grab hold of nothing and hang on until it becomes something! *Faith is vision acted upon.* Jonathan Swift, author of *Gulliver's Travels* said, "Vision is the art of seeing things invisible."[2] Vision is to see things others may not see. Creative prayer is to speak these things into existence through our faith-filled prayers.

7. Decisive Praying

Seventh, and last on my list that day, I explained that strategic-level prayer is *decisive*. In a word, decisive prayer is *conclusive*. This kind of praying, I told the group, represents *a spirit of finality*. I cited Revelation 12:7-12 as a biblical basis for this characteristic. Here we see a conclusive victory in the heavenlies where Satan is dethroned by angelic forces. But those forces only win the victory because God's saints on Earth employ their weapons of "the blood of the Lamb" and "the word of their testimony" (Rev. 12:11). This could only happen, I suggested, through decisive prayer. Such praying is to pray through to a clear conclusion. It is to pray until Satan or his powers are removed (dethroned) in a circumstance or region.

CONFRONTING CAM

Although it is always encouraging as a teacher to see one's students apply your teaching, I was surprised to learn how specifically Agatha led her small prayer band through the seven characteristics that stormy Sunday morning. Step-by-step, methodically and carefully, they prayed and "praised" their way through each aspect.

Agatha later told me they first began by praying *authoritatively*, just as I had suggested on my list. They confidently prayed through the various Scriptures I had given for the point and added others that came to their minds. They prayed with *a spirit of audacity*, an expression they had to translate into its Cantonese equivalent (Cantonese being the dialect they prayed in that morning). According to Agatha, they spoke with authority into the physical atmosphere over Hong Kong.

Then, their prayer became *combative*, the second characteristic on the list. They were aggressive as they sought to pray with *a spirit of militancy*. To the team, this was combat, real warfare, and they saw themselves as a small army strategizing for a victory.

Agatha's intercessors then looked at characteristic three and asked God to give them *a spirit of determination*. They intended to pray with *intensity*. They were reminded of the promise I had shared from James 5:16 (*KJV*) that "effectual fervent prayer" of righteous people produces results. Soon they were praying fervently with a determined intensity. They sensed something was happening in the heavenlies. Little did they suspect what was already transpiring. Just a few miles away, at Hong Kong's weather observatory, meteorologists began to see strange behavior coming from Typhoon Cam.

Back in Agatha's "war room," intercessors kept praying. Now their praying became *confrontive*. They looked at my description of *a spirit of tenacity* and searched for a Cantonese equivalent. Soon they were praying with tenacity, confronting Satan for attempting to disrupt the conference. To them, Typhoon Cam was the mountain, and they were commanding it to move!

Cam was already in trouble. But Agatha's intercessors were not finished yet. Item five on the list was *comprehensive* prayer. So they asked the Holy Spirit to help them focus their prayers with *a spirit of totality*. In the moments that followed they listened and prayed (and prayed and listened), as they pressed in to seek God even more comprehensively regarding Cam and the conference.

SPLITTING THE 8

When they came to characteristic six on the list, *creative prayer*, something unique happened. Initially uncertain as to how to apply this, a member of the group remembered Paul's words, God "quickeneth the dead, and calleth those things which be not as though they were" (Rom. 4:17, *KJV*). Faith began to build within the small team. They sought God for a picture or vision of how to pray.

Suddenly, one of the intercessors saw a gigantic 8 in her mind—the same level as the approaching storm. She knew that if somehow the Signal 8 could be lowered to a Signal 3, transportation could resume. In the natural, this seemed an impossibility.

Then, quite unexpectedly, the intercessor pictured a gigantic hand slicing the huge 8 in half. The left half fell to the ground. A 3 remained standing! She told the group what she had seen, and soon they were moving their hands up and down, symbolically splitting the 8.

The team knew this was a prophetic picture of impending victory. Quickly they moved to the last item on the list—*decisive* prayer. They prayed with *a spirit of finality*, praising God for the coming miracle. In actuality, it was happening in that moment.

At our hotel, Dee and I had moved back to our room on the 16th floor. We wondered when this dreadful storm would hit. However, there was no sign of it. Everything was calm. But because it was now almost 2:00 P.M., I was convinced the conference would be canceled. It was just too late for all the attendees to gather, even if the storm fizzled.

Then the phone rang. It was Agatha. Someone was coming immediately to take us to the meeting. Amazingly, at 2:10 P.M. Cam disappeared. It did not just move, it disappeared! In minutes (not hours) Cam had been lowered from a Signal 8 to a 3. It did not happen gradually but straight from an 8 to a 3. The 8, indeed, had been sliced in half.

As we headed to the final session I wondered how many would attend, since public transportation had just resumed. I soon learned that participants had been watching the weather carefully, and the moment the Signal 3 was announced, they headed for the conference. I was amazed. Every seat was taken.

Worship began promptly at 3:00 P.M. At 3:20 P.M., Agatha came to the microphone to announce that the

Hong Kong Weather Observatory had just issued a bulletin. Typhoon Cam had completely dissipated. It was gone! Agatha later explained that a storm of this magnitude is usually followed by days of heavy rain. But following Cam's "disappearance," there was not even a sprinkle. Even the Signal 3 announced at 2:10 P.M. lasted only about one hour and 10 minutes. Then all signals were lowered to normal. According to Agatha, this was unprecedented!

BUILDING A NEW WALL FOR CHINA

In that final session I was able to pray personally for several hundred intercessors. It was obvious that God had something significant planned for this meeting that almost did not happen. As Agatha's intercessors prayed earlier that day, *a river of God's supremacy* began to flow in Hong Kong. There is little doubt that their praying was prophetic. If prophecy is to "speak before" or "to declare in front of," the intercessory worship of that stormy morning surely was prophetic. It declared God's power "in front of" as well as "before" Typhoon Cam.

The manner in which Agatha's team prophetically penetrated a storm many miles away reminded me of prophets, like Ezekiel and Elijah in ancient times, who prophesied against mountains, valleys, high places and even idols. In the case of Agatha's intercessors, they prophesied against a storm. And they did it through intercessory worship.

Significantly, that September conference in Hong Kong gave birth to a Harp and Bowl Intercessory Worship Conference on Easter weekend the following year, 2000. It was the first such conference for Hong Kong and has now become an annual Easter event. Most recently, believers from more than 150 churches are helping sustain several 24-hour-a-day "walls of prayer" that have been formed. Each "wall" involves intercessors praying for 168 hours in one week's time, which means each wall is covered in prayer 24 hours a day.

This prayer vision is rapidly spreading from Hong Kong across mainland China. Through the ministry of Every Home for Christ, which has led literature evangelism campaigns in more than 1,300 cities and towns in mainland China, these "watchmen walls" are beginning to spread through China's massive networks of house churches. (Some researchers suggest there may be as many as 100 million believers in these Chinese house churches.)

When astronauts first orbited the globe in the 1960s, they reported that the only man-made structure visible from outer space was the Great Wall of China. Soon God may look down and see a much more formidable wall.

Every Home for Christ, together with several other strategic ministries, is setting a goal of enlisting at least one complete wall of 168 hours of prayer in every major Chinese city of 100,000 or more people in the next decade. (That would involve 2,476 cities.) This would create a new wall for China; in this case, a wall of prayer potentially mobilizing hundreds of thousands of hours of annual intercession.

As is typical of great movements of prayer, they are almost always born from prayer itself, usually by a handful of praying vanguards (frontline warriors) like Agatha's intercessors who battled those invisible forces that stormy Hong Kong morning.

There was, indeed, something of a penetrating dimension to the prophetic intercessory worship of that small band of Hong Kong warriors in September 1999. I believe they released a *river of God's supremacy* that will ultimately flow out to that region of the world. They also may have given birth to a prayer movement for China that is unparalleled in history. A great wall, indeed, is rising.

THUNDER FROM THE THRONE

RIVER OF PRODUCTIVITY: THE PREVAILING DIMENSION OF INTERCESSORY WORSHIP

It was not the first time I was baffled by a thought, even though I was certain it was from God. The words were clear—but the meaning confusing. *Lift My praise against the impurity of the signal!*

What signal? And what about it was impure?

Over the years I have tried to discern when God is really

speaking or when it is just me. The "just me" part of seeking divine guidance can be a little scary. Some believers, I am sure, fearing the risk of the "just me" syndrome, give up entirely. What I have concluded from years of trying *to listen* in prayer is—*in listening you learn*. And there does come a time, at least eventually, when you sense in your heart that God really is speaking.

I was certain of it that day. It was just past 2:30 in the afternoon, as I worshiped and prayed with about 80 intercessors. We had gathered in a television studio of a growing Christian television ministry. It was November 6, 1985. At the request of the their leader, I was directing a special afternoon of prayer for the blessing and extension of their ministry. I was pleased that their leader saw the necessity of prayer, and I was glad to participate.

The leader had intended to be with us most of the afternoon; but when I arrived at noon to begin the session, he told me that something serious had come up. It related to a "legal" question, and he would be unable to join us until it was resolved.

BLENDING FOR BATTLE

The plan that afternoon had been for me to provide several brief periods of instruction, followed by prolonged times of prayer and worship. In those days I did not refer to this as *intercessory worship,* and I was yet to link the harp and bowl symbolism of Revelation 5:8-10 to ministry occasions like this, but looking back I realize this is what we were engaged in.

At the outset of the afternoon, I explained that we not only needed to spend ample time in focused prayer for various issues, but that we should saturate these prayers with concentrated worship. Quickly we moved into a specific time devoted to "directed" worship. Soon voices were blending in a unique "worship agreement," as various participants spoke their words of praise and adoration. Little did I know that our voices of worship soon would be blending for battle in a most unusual manner.

Earlier I had suggested that we not only praise God but that we also declare God's praises over specific issues for which we intended to intercede. I reminded the intercessors of something that was becoming foundational to my thinking in those formative days: *God establishes His throne where people praise Him.* It is a theme I particularly highlighted in the first book of my Delight trilogy, *Heights of Delight.*

King David, in one of his many psalms, referred to God as One who "inhabitest" (Ps. 22:3, *KJV*) the praises of Israel,

His people. The literal Hebrew translation of this passage suggests that God is enthroned or sits amid (or upon) the praises of His people. As I mentioned in *Heights of Delight*, the essence of the original meaning may best be summed up by the literal Japanese translation, "When God's people praise Him, He brings a big chair and sits there."

> If we praise God *over* a need, He will become enthroned *in* that need.

All this, I explained to those intercessors, suggests that if we praise God *over* a need, He will become enthroned *in* that need. And if God is enthroned *in* a need, it would seem certain that His presence would produce victory. At least that was my developing theology and theory of Psalm 22:3 at the time.

That is when I heard this strange directive, "Lift my praise against the impurity of the signal!"

I had no doubt God was speaking, but what did He mean? I was glad others were worshiping at the time because it provided me with a few quiet moments to think about how to respond. Unfortunately, my first impressions of what this might mean missed the mark completely.

A STRANGE DIRECTIVE

I sensed that whatever it was that God intended for us to do was in some way related to the television signal flowing out through that ministry. The fact that something was impure about the signal troubled me. And I was unsure as to how to say this to those who were worshiping with me that day.

Because there had been serious moral failure with certain television evangelists at the time, I immediately assumed that this was somehow related. Perhaps someone else, also living in sin, was broadcasting regularly on that very network. In God's eyes, so I reasoned, this would pollute the whole signal. This assumption proved to be entirely wrong, but it was an understandable interpretation at the time.

Fortunately, God quickly reminded me that it was not my responsibility to understand every detail of His directive; I was only to obey. So cautiously I explained to the group the unusual directive.

Thankfully, I did not tell them what I thought it meant. Instead, I told them exactly what the Lord had told me, "Lift My praise against the impurity of the signal!" I even cautioned them not to draw their own conclusions. "Let's just respond in obedience," I suggested.

Although I had believed for some time that our praise enthrones God in situations, this clearly seemed different. How, for example, does one declare God's praises into an invisible television signal? And if there is something impure about that signal, how would our praise affect it? My theological musings were again bogging me down.

I finally gave in and simply led the group in prayers of praise (what I now know as intercessory worship), inviting them to join me in verbal declarations of God's nature and character. I told them I did not know exactly how we were to proceed, so they should not feel bad if they were also a little confused. "Let's just lift God's praise against what He knows He means by the 'impurity of the signal,'" I suggested.

PRAISE THAT PREVAILS

Thus, our intercessory worship began. I found myself declaring things like, "God, I praise you in all your greatness and majesty, and I enthrone you in this television signal." We even sang several worship choruses. As the group sang, I spoke into the microphone declaring, "Lord, we sing these praises into the signal of this ministry." I did not know if this was exactly right, but it was all I knew to do.

Frankly, worshiping and praying in this manner seemed a little awkward. Usually, worship is simply to praise God; that is, to adore and exalt Him for who He is. Prayer, of course, is to ask God for things. Prayer becomes intercession when we ask for things as they relate to others. But in this case, we were praising God "against" something—at least to the extent that we were enthroning Him in this specific circumstance. We were, to be sure, praising God—but we were doing it in reference to that impure signal.

The intercessory worship continued for almost 45 minutes as various people spoke out their declarations of praise and prayer. At times we also gathered in small groups to more intensively focus prayer on the impure signal.

Then, suddenly, everyone began clapping. I was not sure why. As the spontaneous clapping continued, I felt led to shout boldly into the microphone, "We lift the praises of our God against you, impure signal, and declare that you are being cleansed even as we worship."

It sounds odd, to say the least. Still, no one present had any doubt something unique was happening. Everyone could sense it. Soon we were praising God with a sense of imminent victory.

Just then the head of the ministry walked into the studio. "I don't know exactly how all of you have been praying today," he explained. "But I can tell you this—in the last 30 minutes I have seen one of the greatest miracles our ministry has ever experienced."

A BOLT OF POWER

The leader explained why he had been unable to join us for much of the afternoon. An incident had arisen concerning one of their television stations hundreds of miles away. He had been on the telephone with attorneys trying to resolve the issue. The problem had begun about six months earlier when the ministry acquired a large transmission tower near this particular station. It would help them broadcast to a greatly expanded area with several hundred thousand additional homes. But there was a problem. The previous owners of the tower had leased it to a "heavy metal" rock and roll station and their lease still had six months remaining.

What especially troubled this Christian leader was the nature of the music broadcast from this station 24 hours a day. It was not just ordinary rock and roll but a new, unusually vile, satanic-inspired heavy metal music. It openly exalted and honored Satan. Satan, he told us, was not only freely exalted in the music, but rape, murder, incest and even suicide were encouraged.

Herein lay the problem. This television ministry now owned the tower. Attached near the top of the tower were two microwave dishes, less than 30 feet apart, transmitting 24 hours a day. One was broadcasting Christian television 24 hours a day and the other the songs of Satan, also 24 hours daily.

The leader's discussions with his attorneys that day had examined what steps might be taken to cancel the remaining six months of the lease to this rock station. The attorneys, however, having studied the lease, explained that nothing could be done without a resulting lawsuit of potentially significant impact. And, the attorneys advised, the television ministry would almost certainly lose.

During these legal discussions, just a short distance away in the television studio, God gave us our strange direction to lift praises against the impurity of the signal.

The leader repeated himself, "I'm not sure how you've been praying, but God certainly has heard you. Less than a half hour ago a thunderstorm formed over the mountain where our tower stands, and that tower was struck by lightning."

He laughed as he asked, "Would you like to know which of the two transmission dishes was hit?"

The intercessors began clapping even before he could answer. God had thundered from His throne. They knew it had been the rock station's dish that had been hit by lightning. Further, this bolt of power did not jump to the ministry's television dish. It traveled down through the thick wires into the heavy metal rock station's on-site control room, completely destroying that station's broadcasting equipment. The radio station was permanently put off the air.

PROPHETIC PRODUCTIVITY

A year later I traveled to the city where all this happened to conduct a School of Prayer. During the teaching I related the television ministry's story as an example of the power of praise in spiritual warfare. During the break, a man in his 30s approached me. "Thanks, Dick," he said, "for telling the story about that transmission tower. If you need someone to verify its accuracy, I can!"

He quickly explained that he owned a company that installed and repaired transmission equipment like I had been describing. In fact, his company had been called the day after the tower had been struck by lightning, and he had personally removed the dish from the tower. "Not only did I climb up the tower and remove that dish," he explained. "I still have it. I just never realized I had a miracle sitting in my garage."

There is little doubt that the intercessory worship in that television studio was both prophetic and prevailing. During those unique moments, 80 intercessors experienced the flow of *God's river of productivity*. Said simply: Prophetic intercessory worship produces results.

I saw in this unique experience several factors regarding the power of prophetic intercessory worship, especially as it releases God's *river of productivity*.

1. Intercessory Worship Exalts God

Productive intercessory worship *exalts* God. This reality is central to all that God showed me in writing my Delight trilogy. The psalmist declared, "Thou art my God, and I will praise thee: thou art my God, I will exalt thee" (Ps. 118:28, *KJV*). The television-tower encounter and resulting victory occurred because God was exalted in that circumstance. Only the Holy Spirit could have known all the details involved. We could not have prayed all-knowingly to remove the polluting transmission dish because we did not have this information. But God knew, and when He was exalted in that situation, victory was assured.

2. Intercessory Worship Exercises Authority

Productive intercessory worship *exercises authority*. Interestingly, according to Matthew's Gospel, the first assignment Christ gave His disciples when He first commissioned them was not specifically to preach—that was to come later on their list of directives—rather, it was to exercise authority against demonic powers. Matthew records, "Jesus called his twelve disciples to him and gave them authority to cast out evil spirits and to heal every kind of disease and illness" (Matt. 10:1, *NLT*). He goes on to say: "As you go, preach . . . 'The kingdom of heaven is near'" (Matt. 10:7). Thus, prophetic intercessory worship, by exercising Christ's authority, prepares people to receive the gospel.

3. Intercessory Worship Eliminates Strongholds

Productive intercessory worship *eliminates strongholds*. This, I believe, is what occurred that day in the television studio. Something happened similar to what Christ said was necessary to seize a stronghold. He said, "No one can enter a strong man's house and plunder his goods, unless he first binds the strong man" (Mark 3:27, *NKJV*). That day in the studio, praise bound the strongman. In this sense, praise can be as much a weapon as prayer can. Paul wrote: "The weapons we fight with are not the weapons of the world. On the contrary, they have divine power to demolish strongholds" (2 Cor. 10:4). Any spiritual discipline that resists or restrains demonic powers is a weapon. Praise was precisely that as we worshiped God in that television studio.

4. Intercessory Worship Encompasses Nations

Productive intercessory worship *encompasses nations*. The sweep of prevailing, prophetic prayer ultimately impacts the whole world. We recall how Revelation 5:8-10, with the harp and bowl symbolism, immediately precedes a new song of a global harvest. The song pictures the redeemed coming "from every tribe and language and people and nation" (Rev. 5:9). There is no mistaking that the intercessory worship pictured in this passage of the harp (worship) and bowl (intercession) is connected to this massive ingathering of the redeemed.

Most interesting is where the harvest first began. It began in the Upper Room on the Day of Pentecost (see Acts 2:1-11). Although perhaps not identified as such, this too involved intercessory worship. The ingredients of intercessory worship clearly were present. These disciples were continually in prayer, which in a sense was like the filling of their "bowls." This happened while they engaged in fervent worship, which is equivalent to employing their "harps" (see Acts 1:14; 2:11). That this combination touched the nations is clear. Visitors from numerous nearby nations heard and understood these worshipers declaring God's praises in each of their languages:

> Believing in a big God, which is enhanced through intercessory worship, builds a prayer confidence that anticipates big answers.

Godly Jews from many nations were living in Jerusalem at that time. When they heard this sound [like the roaring of a mighty windstorm], they came running to see what it was all about, and they were bewildered to hear their own languages being spoken by the believers (Acts 2:5-6, *NLT*).

Coming yet closer to the Upper Room, these visitors declared, " . . . we all hear these people speaking in our own languages about the wonderful things God has done!" (Acts 2:11, *NLT*). So from the very birthing of the Church, supernatural worship has impacted the nations because of the wonderful things God has done.

5. Intercessory Worship Expects Answers

Productive intercessory worship *expects answers*. Faith flows more freely when we saturate our intercession with zealous worship. Worship creates a climate for the kind of faith Jesus described: "Therefore I tell you, whatever you ask for in prayer, believe that you have received it, and it will be yours" (Mark 11:24).

Believing in a big God, which is enhanced through intercessory worship, builds a prayer confidence that anticipates big answers. Worship-saturated prayer encourages a confidence like John described: "And we can be confident that he will listen to us whenever we ask him for anything in line with his will. And if we know he is listening when we make our requests, we can be sure that he will give us what we ask for" (1 John 5:14-15, *NLT*). Worship creates a climate for confident praying!

A FEAST OF JOY

This kind of confidence led to one of the most unusual answers to prayer I recall hearing about during my 25 years of involvement with Every Home for Christ. Two of our workers in Fiji had traveled by commercial boat to one of Fiji's distant islands. (The Fiji chain consists of 106 inhabited islands scattered over tens of thousands of square miles of ocean.)

The two evangelists had only enough funds for their travel to the island. But they knew of the hospitality of Fijians and had already contacted the local pastor with whom they had agreed to work in taking the gospel in printed form to every household on the island. From experience they knew that God had His unique ways of providing. He always had provided for them. They were sure He would sustain them until they completed their assignment in two to three weeks. Christians there, no doubt, would help them with their return fare.

Upon their arrival, the evangelists met the young pastor and his wife. The woman was obviously in the last stages of pregnancy. It was to be their first child. Little did the workers know she would give birth that very night, in a room adjacent to where they would be sleeping.

The pastor was very apologetic as they arrived. He informed the workers that due to recent storms in the area, no fish had been caught for several days. (Fish were their primary source of food.) Thus, the couple was unable to serve them any dinner—a clear embarrassment in so hospitable a culture. The young men just accepted this as another opportunity to fast, something they usually did on a regular basis anyway.

Just after midnight the workers were abruptly awakened by the groans of the pastor's wife as she went into labor. There would be no sleep that night. By morning a beautiful baby boy had been born.

Now, according to Fijian tradition, this posed an interesting dilemma for the workers. Visitors of a Fijian family, when a firstborn child arrives, must always provide a gift. These workers, of course, had no money for such a gift. Now they would be the ones apologizing.

As the sun rose, one of the workers decided to walk along the beach to pray and worship. Soon he was wading in the surf, worshiping the God he knew had never failed to provide. Suddenly he saw something bobbing in the waves. He could not miss it. The color was striking—a bright orange. Oddly, the object also seemed to jerk about, as if something inside was causing this strange movement.

The worshiper waded into the water and began chuckling joyfully. He could not believe what he saw. It was a brand-new plastic tub for bathing infants. He was certain it was new because it still had a price tag attached, $12.95, apparently in New Zealand dollars. (New Zealand is many hundreds of miles across the Pacific from Fiji.) The evangelist could not imagine a more appropriate gift for the new mother.

Yet there was more. The tub was jerking because, inside, flopping about, were two large fish—the most desirable kind caught in those Pacific waters. There would be a feast of joy that night, in more ways than one. What had begun as a day of discouragement had turned into a day of delight. This Fijian evangelist had walked into the surf worshiping and discovered a river—God's *river of productivity*, in which intercessory worship prevails.

THE DARK SIDE OF BALI

RIVER OF DISCOVERY: THE PERCEPTIVE DIMENSION OF INTERCESSORY WORSHIP

As one seasoned traveler said, "From the air, Bali rises fresh and green from the Indian Ocean, a verdant, glistening butterfly against a backdrop of gray."[1] The island is, indeed, one of the most beautiful places on Earth.

Bali is intriguing. It is an island of southern Indonesia, just east of Java, and one of an estimated 17,000 islands in the Indonesian chain. About 3,000 of these are inhabited. Some 210 million people, mostly Muslim, live in this vast archipelago, a chain of islands scattered across 741,052 square miles of the Indian and Pacific Oceans. With its towering mountains, tropical climate and fertile soil, Bali stands out in beauty above them all. Just 90 miles long by 60 miles at its widest point, and not much more than one mile at its narrowest, Bali's beauty has earned it the nickname "the Jewel of the East."

But there is a dark side to Bali. It is like so many places on our planet that are uniquely rich in culture, awe inspiring in its geography and wonderfully inviting to tourists looking for an exotic place to visit for a week or two. But most people have no idea of the power of darkness controlling these regions and the impact of that spiritual darkness as it reaches out to other areas—and, as we saw in the case of Tibet, sometimes touching the entire world.

PROPHETIC PERCEPTION

A friend and prayer strategist, John Robb, who leads World Vision's prayer thrust, believes this is the case with Bali, where he traveled in 1996 with a prayer team of 10 seasoned intercessors from five nations. They met at Besakih,

Bali, with a larger group of 70 Balinese believers and other Christians from neighboring Indonesian islands. Additionally, thousands of other intercessors around the world were supporting the initiative through their prayers, including 40 organizations affiliated with the AD2000 and Beyond Movement's prayer network, plus thousands of praying Christians from Dr. Yonggi Cho's massive congregation of Yoido Full Gospel Church in Seoul, Korea. There were even 340 churches in Sri Lanka that agreed to cover this strategic initiative in prayer.

John and his team learned numerous interesting lessons from their Bali prayer initiative that help us define *the perceptive dimension of intercessory worship* and introduce what I believe to be God's *river of discovery*. At the heart of this dimension is an understanding of what George Otis, Jr., refers to as "informed intercession," something we will examine shortly.

The prophetic, by its very nature, is perceptive. To "perceive" is "to apprehend or observe especially through sight or with the mind." To perceive also means "to understand, discern, comprehend or grasp." "Perception," as a noun, is "the intuitive recognition of a truth or reality." "Intuition," then, is "immediate insight or understanding without conscious reasoning."[2]

When you add to these concepts the supernatural dimension of the Holy Spirit's providing these insights, the result is prophetic perception that releases this *river of discovery*. To me, the channel for the flow of this prophetic river is intercessory worship. Worship enthrones God, thus releasing His power for ready application, while intercession focuses or applies that power to specific needs. The discovery part is the manner in which God reveals exactly how to pray in specific situations. A case in point is the example dealt with in the previous chapter when God revealed that we were to confront the impurity of the transmission signal through praise. In that situation, we were depending on the Holy Spirit to direct God's power, through praise, to the specific nature of the need.

> Worship enthrones God, thus releasing His power for ready application, while intercession focuses or applies that power to specific needs.

Such dependence on the Holy Spirit is not to suggest the intercessor is merely a passive player in such praying—

someone simply waiting for a Spirit-led prompting to intercede for a certain situation and only then gets involved by praying. It seems those who flow best in this river of prophetic discovery are those who do their homework in prayer, which brings us back to the description George Otis, Jr., uses—"informed intercession."

The expression defines itself: the gleaning of accurate information leading to informed intercession. Armies devote considerable time and resources to gathering accurate intelligence, so they will know how to wage war effectively. We, too, need to do our homework for prayer by gathering as much information as possible regarding the focus of our intercession. Then when the prophetic element is added to what our homework has produced, incredible prayer possibilities await us. The power of such praying seems further amplified when saturated with fervent worship. Still, we must do our homework. Preparation for worship-saturated prayer often leads to unusual prophetic perception in prayer.

A BALI PRAYER PRIMER

John Robb understood the importance of informed intercession as he prepared to lead the 1996 Bali prayer initiative.

For several months prior to the journey, John researched all he could about this exotic place, its history, culture, religious beliefs and even the status of Christianity in the island. In a sense, he compiled his own Bali "prayer primer."

According to John, he was specifically searching for two things: (1) What is the identity of the strongman over the island? and (2) How does this strongman maintain his control?

Bali, John explains, is known as *Pulau Dewata*, the "islands of the gods." There are many gods, demons and ancestral spirits worshiped in Bali. But John wondered if there was one specific entity or force that seemed to rise above all the others, one that would fall into the category of a "strong man" like Jesus described in Mark 3:27. If this force could be identified, John felt they could focus prayers on restraining (binding) the influence of this entity and thus "carry off his possessions," which in this case were the souls of the Balinese.

Secondly, John wondered how this strongman maintained his control, because, as John explained to me, that control is the essence of the demonic. The goal of principalities and powers (see Eph. 6:10-12) is to attempt to control and dominate human beings and their institutions.

We saw something of this reality in chapter two in looking at Mark Geppert's conch-shell encounter in Tibet.

What John learned in his research was that Bali is the lone Hindu outpost amid the thousands of islands that make up the largely Muslim Indonesian archipelago. Before Hinduism came to Bali, ancient Indonesians on this small island worshiped what they termed "great native gods" consisting of the sun, mountains and the sea. Additionally, they invoked the souls of their ancestors, who, they believed, descended to dwell on large stones that had been erected for these departed souls. Even today the Balinese believe their gods live upon the mountains as well as in rocks, trees, wind, birds, streams and lakes. They believe Bali literally *belongs* to the gods and that all human beings are but transitory tenants. The gods are the true landowners.

It was into this powerfully demonic climate that the even stronger satanic forces of Buddhism and Hinduism came to Java and Bali in the fifth century. Hinduism eventually gained the upper hand in gleaning the devotion of these ancient Indonesian sun worshipers, and soon they were worshiping Shiva, the Hindu god of destruction, and Surya, the Hindu sun god. These two gods merged into one for the Balinese and are now particularly identified with Bali's highest mountain, Mount Agong, another obvious demonic high place. Shiva/Surya, according to Balinese traditions, represents divinity, which permeates everything. Balinese believe they combine to become the totality of all the forces they call god. As you can see, John learned a lot to help his team pray meaningfully.

Balinese Hindus further believe their existence is a continuous cycle of life, death and rebirth until one reaches the state of *moska*—when the body becomes one with the universe. Obedience to various rituals at different times in one's life supposedly ensures that the person is progressing properly toward this desired and ultimate goal.[3]

Central to these beliefs is their particular worship of Shiva, believed by the Balinese to be the spirit of their very first ancestor. It was Shiva, they say, who made Brahma (another Hindu god) and Brahma who made the world. This leads them to believe that all human beings are descendants of Shiva.

These details further led John Robb to conclude that the strongman of Bali is Shiva/Surya, which really is a human name for some specific demonic principality or authority in the heavenlies (see Eph. 6:10-12). This power, John was convinced, held a firm grip on the people of Bali.

So John felt he had his Mark 3:27 "strong man" even as he continued his research to learn more about how these powers control the Balinese. God clearly was preparing to equip a small cadre of "informed intercessors" for this Bali prayer initiative.

A FORMIDABLE FORCE

In July 1996, the 10 ministry leaders from five nations joined the 70 indigenous spiritual warriors to form a formidable force of informed intercessors to begin the prayer initiative.

When the combined team first met it was clear the prayers of those thousands of supporting intercessors mentioned earlier were taking effect. John Robb reported, "We could feel their prayers as the Spirit of God moved powerfully among us, giving prophetic words and visions about the destiny of the Balinese people and church, and producing times of deep identificational repentance for the woundedness and idolatry of this people."[4]

Identificational repentance, to which John Robb referred, is that aspect of prayerful repentance in which intercessors identify with those of a people or culture, usually from the past, who had sinned deeply but never repented (Daniel, Isaiah, Nehemiah and others in Scripture serve as examples). Identificational repentance is to repent on behalf of their failures and the entry those failures may have provided to allow demonic powers to infiltrate a land or culture.

Such repentance happened at the Bali initiative. Early on in the praying, Indonesian intercessors repented, particularly for idolatry. They also repented for the multitude of covenants made by Balinese Hindu worshipers with false gods like Shiva, the Hindu god of destruction, as well as Surya, the sun god.

One especially noteworthy prophetic insight came during these initial prayers from the late Kjell Sjoberg, one of the pioneers of the spiritual warfare movement in Europe. Sjoberg specifically spoke of the power of the shed blood of Jesus to bring healing to Bali and the absolute necessity of reconciliation in Christ's Body in Bali in order for this to happen. Sjoberg explained,

> God created Bali with a purpose to reveal His own personality and purpose. Satan wants to block God's voice in creation. He has done this most effectively in Bali since the whole island has been sanctified to demon gods. . . . Spiritual strongholds

are no problem for a united church. Therefore the groundwork before spiritual warfare that can be effective always involves reconciliation in the Body of Christ. . . . The deeper we go in repentance, the higher we go in spiritual warfare.[5]

This prophetic statement led to significant repentance. Participants identified with many sins of their various cultures and peoples. For example, a man from Java (a main island of Indonesia) repented of the way his people had mistreated the people of Bali. Then, an Indonesian with Dutch blood asked for forgiveness for the massacres of the Balinese generations before by Dutch colonialists. A male Balinese intercessor repented for the subjugation of the women of Bali. Especially moving was a time when nine Balinese leaders led the entire team in repentance for the worship (idolatry) of "the creation" among the Bali people, something Balinese Christian leadership believes is a major sin of their island.

THE FALL OF ANCIENT COVENANTS

This spirit of repentance soon was taken beyond the walls of the prayer meeting in Besakih and into the surrounding community. Almost 50 of the intercessors participated in a quiet, low-profile prayer walk that included a visit to Bali's main Hindu shrine where several Balinese leaders, acting on behalf of their people, prayerfully broke the covenants the ancient inhabitants of Bali had made with Shiva/Surya. There was considerable weeping, repentance and intercession, even though it was done in public. Clearly God was moving, and the brokenness of these Balinese believers seemed to be breaking something of a stronghold in the heavenlies.

Soon, four smaller teams, each led by a local Balinese Christian, were dispatched to various additional locations, including major temples and places of historic massacres and bloodshed.

John Robb joined a team that journeyed to the southernmost temple in Bali, Ulu Watu. Outside that temple they prayerfully sought God to break the powers of darkness over it, including its obvious occultist link to other shrines and temples throughout Bali. Not long after their prayers at Ulu Watu, this temple was struck by lightning and burned, causing over $100,000 worth of damage. It was a huge sum to the people of Bali. A local newspaper lamented, "Why did our god allow this to happen to his temple?"

Amazingly, falling logs struck two other temples in the mountains of Bali, both of which had visits by prayer teams. A short time later the government of Bali destroyed yet another major temple that had been prayed over, in this case for developmental purposes. Additionally, since this prayer initiative, the mother temple of all of Bali temples, the one in Besakih where those initial prayers of repentance occurred, has been closed to all outside visitors. No explanation for the closure has been given.

At the end of the Bali initiative, everyone involved in the prayer thrust sensed a noticeable change in the spiritual atmosphere over the island. This was especially true of local leaders. They said they could feel the oppression lifting.

The following morning a minor earthquake shook Bali as an almost symbolic gesture that God had begun to shake the island with His presence. The earthquake reminded John of two prayer pictures that intercessors saw before the initiative began. One saw a dark blanket being rolled back off the island as God's light began to shine over it. Another had seen a mushroom cloud of darkness being lifted from the island.

In the months that immediately followed, there were specific signs of spiritual renewal among nominal

Christians in Bali. Churches reported a growth in the number of healing and deliverance meetings, something so needed in this dark island. There was also a noticeable increase in responsiveness to the gospel by unbelievers. In one particularly resistant region, an area where one of the intercessory teams had gone for prayer, a local pastor baptized 15 new believers—a true miracle for this dark area.

In another place where pastors began a monthly united prayer meeting, an especially strange phenomenon occurred. When the Indonesian government began to build a 400-foot statue honoring still another Hindu god, Vishnu, the local pastors made it a target of their prayers. A short time later the statue's head mysteriously caught fire and was destroyed. Interestingly, such phenomena often preceded a greater openness to the gospel. For Bali, all of this could well represent the beginnings of a spiritual breakthrough.

A PICTURE OF PRECIOUS STONES

John Robb more recently reported similar results from intercessors' initiatives in Africa. Two accounts are particularly noteworthy. Both involved elements of prophetic intercession and worship.

The Democratic Republic of the Congo, formerly Zaire, is a nation that has been devastated for decades by corruption, war and disease. After the late and unusually corrupt President Sese Seko Mobutu was driven from power in 1997, 60-year-old Laurent Kabila became president. President Kabila opposed any peace process in the region. But within months of a prayer initiative similar to the thrust held in Bali, Kabila was assassinated (in January 2001). His son Joseph, in his 30s, replaced President Kabila. Most Congolese expected more of the same, but a surprise awaited. It soon was reported that Joseph Kabila had accepted Christ and was being discipled by a local evangelical pastor. Another source said that the younger Kabila, who openly advocates peace and reconciliation, has been transporting prayer leaders from throughout the country to the nation's capitol, Kinshasa, for special prayer. The nation is still terribly troubled, but intercession is having an effect.

Yet another African intercessor's initiative seems to have planted significant seeds for transformation. This one took place in the devastated central-African nation of Rwanda. Less than a decade ago Rwanda was plagued with one of history's worst examples of genocide. In 1994, more than 500,000 were slaughtered in the conflict between Hutu and Tutsi peoples. Most of those killed were Tutsis. At a recent follow-up intercessor's summit held in Bujumbura, Burundi, leaders from Rwanda reported that signs of transformation had begun. The government was now openly promoting national unity and reconciliation. They were asking both the churches of Rwanda and the population at large to give input. All of this began *after* the first prayer summit.

Leaders also reported that Hutu rebels, instead of being killed by the military—something everyone had expected—were now being given food and clothing and were even allowed to visit their families after hiding for years in the jungle. Although the region still has its troubles, this was an especially unusual indication of true reconciliation and the beginning of the restoration of basic human rights in Rwanda.

One unique result of that first Rwandan prayer initiative involved a prophetic promise given through one of the intercessors. She declared that as intentional acts of reconciliation were undertaken there would come the discovery of "precious stones." After that prayer initiative, and those initial steps toward reconciliation, mineral deposits were discovered that have particular value in the production of certain computer components. God's *river of discovery* not only led to a heightened perception in informed intercession, but it also flowed to a discovery of mineral deposits that may potentially bless the people of an entire nation. God's promise of healing the land if His people humble themselves seems to be happening in East Africa (see 2 Chron. 7:14). God is uniquely blessing the land itself. And prophetic intercessory worship has played a role.

GRANDMA'S SURPRISE

RIVER OF LIBERTY: THE PERSONAL DIMENSION OF INTERCESSORY WORSHIP

I call her Grandma Anna. No one knows her real name for sure. I chose this pseudonym because this Asian grandmother reminds me of the elderly prophetess, Anna, of Luke 2:36-37. My Anna was a 90-year-old convert from the "least evangelized" Isaan people group in northern Thailand. Her people, about 17 million who speak the Lao/Isaan language, are classified as "least evangelized" because less than 5 percent of their population has been converted.

One day, as Anna sat quietly on her straw mat listening to the leader of her small Bible-study group, she had a strange urge. It was a surprise that would stun the group. The 90-year-old saint soon would step into God's prophetic *river of liberty* and, in so doing, open the heavens for a remarkable release of God's presence among her people. Anna's act introduces us to *the personal dimension of intercessory worship* and reveals how our individual worship can have unusual prophetic implications. (More about Grandma Anna's surprise in a moment.)

KEEPING IT PERSONAL

All that might be said about the various dimensions of intercessory worship mentioned on these pages, and how they might impact those around us as well as distant nations, has relatively little significance if its principles cannot be applied personally. To King David, worship was always personal. He said, "One thing I ask of the LORD, this is what I seek: that I may dwell in the house of the LORD all the days of my life, to gaze upon the beauty of the LORD and to seek him in his temple" (Ps. 27:4).

Notice the expressions "I ask," "I seek" and "that I may dwell." Knowing God and worshiping Him was David's supreme passion. And it was personal.

Years ago while reading through the Psalms, I was fascinated by the repeated requests for personal blessings. I counted at least 50 occasions where David and other psalmists used expressions like "lead me," "strengthen me," "guide me," "heal me," "revive me" and so forth. Psalm 143, for example, has at least nine such appeals. This suggests that even as we develop prayer of an intercessory nature (that which focuses on others), there is nothing wrong with seeking personal blessing.

> As we develop prayer of an intercessory nature (that which focuses on others), there is nothing wrong with seeking personal blessing.

Yet David especially understood that God's presence was the greatest of all personal blessings. Another of his psalms says, "O God, you are my God; I earnestly search for you. My soul thirsts for you; my whole body longs for you. . . . I have seen you in your sanctuary. . . . how

I praise you! I will honor you. . . . You satisfy me. . . . I will praise you with songs of joy" (Ps. 63:1-5, *NLT*).

Notice the expressions "I earnestly search," "my soul thirsts for you," "my whole body longs for you," "I will honor you," "You satisfy me" and "I will praise you." There are 12 personal references to being blessed in just these five verses. Although David led worship corporately, he also kept it personal.

Also consider Paul's challenge to make worship both corporate and personal: "Be filled with the Spirit. Speak to one another with psalms, hymns and spiritual songs. Sing and make music in your heart to the Lord" (Eph. 5:18-19).

On the one hand, Paul says, "Speak to one another with psalms, hymns and spiritual songs," which is corporate worship. But then he says, *"Sing and make music in your heart to the Lord"* (emphasis added), which involves a personal dimension of worship. And sometimes this can become uniquely prophetic, which brings us back to Grandma Anna.

REVERENT DETERMINATION

I was first introduced to Grandma Anna by Paul DeNeui, who wrote in an issue of *Missions Frontiers* that featured indigenous worship in church planting. Paul described an experience of missionaries Jim and Joan Gustafson who had gone to Thailand in 1971. Their mission was to minister among the nearly 20 million least-evangelized peoples of northern Thailand.[1]

According to the Gustafsons, the primary forms most Thai Christians have adopted to express their worship are western imports. Thus, the average unconverted Thai, when viewing typical church worship, would say Christianity is a foreigner's religion.

Because the Gustafsons particularly wanted to evangelize the Isaan people of northern Thailand, and do so in an Isaan cultural context of music and dance, they began praying about how to accomplish this. Central to such worship would be the use of the Isaan *kaen* (bamboo panpipes) along with their traditional dance. But this had its challenges. When Christianity had first come to northern Thailand, converts were taught to worship only in the Central Thai language and in a Western way. In fact, many Thai Christians still associate the use of the kaen and Isaan dance with worship of animistic spirits. Amazingly, in earlier days, even teaching people to worship in their own local language (in this case, Lao/Isaan) was considered radical.

Then a breakthrough came. It happened with Grandma's surprise. During one of the local language Bible studies, as a small group of students sat in a circle on straw mats listening intently, Grandma Anna slowly stood up, unannounced. With a look of reverent determination she moved to the center of the circle. In an instant Anna was dancing freely in the traditional Isaan fashion. Her thin arms were waving gracefully as her fingers moved expressively.

In deliberate steps Anna silently swayed in worship. There was no music. Onlookers were stunned. Most in the group believed the use of traditional Thai worship was satanic. No Isaan believer had ever danced like this in their worship. They were aghast.

Finally, one shouted, "Grandma, sit down! What do you think you're doing?"

Without a pause, Anna declared, "You don't tell your old grandma to sit down. I'm 90 years old, and I'm just thanking the Lord."

PANPIPES OF PRAISE

Her dance was pure and personal. But even more, it was prophetic. Something broke in the heavenlies over northern Thailand that night. The missionaries reported that everything changed in their worship following Grandma's surprise. Isaan dance soon became a part of their worship, and indigenous Isaan music quickly followed. Now the unique melodious kaen panpipes were sending melodies of praise heavenward. These panpipes, once used to worship satanic spirits, had become panpipes of praise. One Isaan worshiper, defending the use of the kaen, queried, "Why can't we use the kaen to praise God? We used our same mouth to worship the spirits before. Does this mean we need to get a new mouth to praise God now?"

Before long, Isaan believers developed their own hymnody (indigenous songs). One recent Isaan chorus focuses on Jesus, the Word:

> From the Heavenly City the Word came down.
> He was born right here where we live.
> We Isaan people have happiness now.
> He loves us and that will not change!
> The Lord Jesus Christ, the victor over death,
> Is born in our cultural forms.
> Listen to the sounds of the flute and the drum.
> All Isaan rejoices in Him![2]

Grandma Anna's act of worship, initially a personal desire to honor the Lord, had prophetic implications. Through her dance, Anna stepped into a *river of liberty* and released something of the flow of that river among her people. Soon, far more Isaan people were able to receive the gospel in their cultural context. Those who found Christ were then able to worship the Lord in the liberty of that same indigenous context.

TAKING A FEW STEPS

How does one *step* into this *river of liberty*? The answer, I believe, begins with that lone word—"step." Grandma Anna's prophetic act began with a single step. It took her toward the center of the circle during that Bible study. It became a step into God's *river of liberty*.

Recently God has been dealing with the leadership of our ministry, Every Home for Christ, about His taking us "a new way" toward accomplishing our goal of mobilizing Christ's Body globally to reach every home in the world with a presentation of the gospel. Although the goal may sound impossibly ambitious, in EHC's 55-year history, such campaigns already have occurred in 191 nations where over 2 billion printed gospel messages have been planted. The ministry has been encouraged by 28 million followed-up decision cards, and the planting of more than 43,000 New Testament fellowships, called Christ Groups.

But even though we have seen these gratifying results, the daunting task ahead is to reach every home among remote people groups and in highly restricted areas such as Middle Eastern Islamic nations. New ideas with new strategies are necessary to accomplish this objective. Something prophetic is required.

I thought particularly about a familiar Old Testament lesson where Joshua leads God's people across the Jordan River and into their land of promise (see Josh. 3:1-17). Although it was a corporate crossing, it became personal to everyone who journeyed.

For three days the Israelites had camped at the Jordan before their crossing. Interestingly, in the same way that Israel miraculously fled Egypt with the parting of the Red Sea, they would now enter the Promised Land with the parting of the Jordan River. But first there were critical requirements.

Joshua sent his leaders throughout the camp with this directive:

When you see the Levitical priests carrying the Ark of the Covenant of the LORD your God, follow them. Since you have never traveled this way before, they will guide you. Stay about a half mile behind them, keeping a clear distance between you and the Ark. Make sure you don't come any closer (Josh. 3:3-4, *NLT*).

Joshua added this especially vital assignment: "Purify yourselves, for tomorrow the LORD will do great wonders among you" (v. 5, *NLT*).

God was clearly taking His people a new way. Joshua had said, "You have never traveled this way before" (v. 4, *NLT*)!

Essentially, God's people were given a fivefold commissioning that seems applicable today according to this passage in Joshua:

1. Be Ready!

The commissioning begins, "When you see the Levitical priests carrying the Ark" (v. 3, *NLT*). There's an alertness suggested here. The people are told to keep watch for the "priests carrying the Ark." They knew that at any moment something might happen. This shows us that we too must ready ourselves for the new way. God is preparing new opportunities for His children. Are we ready to receive them?

2. Be Responsive!

The Israelites are next told, "When you see the Levitical priests carrying the Ark . . . follow them" (v. 3, NLT). Response must follow readiness. There is little doubt that God intends to move upon His people in fresh ways—even new and extraordinary ways—in these last days. In ancient times the Ark of the Covenant represented the dwelling place of God, His presence. Thus the people were being told that when they saw God's presence begin to "move," they were to respond. To get to God's new place for us, we must move as He leads us.

> God is preparing new opportunities for His children. Are we ready to receive them?

3. Be Receptive!

Something fascinates me in the text about listening and receiving what God "shows" through the Levitical priests. Without this, there is no new way. Note specifically, "When you see the Levitical priests carrying the Ark . . . *follow them*. Since you have never traveled this way before, *they will guide you*" (vv. 3-4, NLT, emphasis added).

I believe the New Testament equivalent to the Old Testament Levitical priest is the prophetic intercessor.

A Levitical priest, for one thing, interceded before God on behalf of the people. The New Testament intercessor also clearly fulfills this function. A Levitical priest also spoke God's messages "before the people," which involved the prophetic. We recall that both the Hebrew and Greek words for "prophesy" mean "to speak before," meaning to declare a fact in advance of it happening, or speaking a word from the Lord *before* God's people.

To me as a leader of a global evangelism ministry, this suggested that we need a heightened regard for those with a prophetic ministry of intercession. We need intercessors to help us cover our planning and activities with their prayers, as well as to help us hear from the Lord in our strategizing.

4. Be Repentant!

There is little doubt the heart of this lesson comes in the words of Joshua: "Purify yourselves, for tomorrow the LORD will do great wonders among you" (v. 5, *NLT*). The *New International Version* begins, "Consecrate yourselves . . . " and the *King James Version* says, "Sanctify yourselves. . . ." Each of these expressions suggests ridding ourselves of everything impure before God, so we might move forward unhindered toward His promise. Repentance is the key to this process, whether described as purification, sanctification or consecration. It is to change when change is required. To repent means "to turn from."[3]

5. Be Released!

The final phase in the process of moving in a new way is reduced simply to stepping out. God tells Joshua, "Give these instructions to the priests who are carrying the Ark of the Covenant: 'When you reach the banks of the Jordan River, take a few steps into the river and stop'" (Josh. 3:8, *NLT*).

Everything remarkable accomplished in our walk *with* Jesus begins by taking a few steps *in* Him. Then we must willingly wait for Him to act. Consider Joshua's dilemma. His priests stepped into the Jordan at the worst time of the year to attempt such a crossing. The Bible says, "Now it was the harvest season, and the Jordan was overflowing its banks" (Josh. 3:15, *NLT*).

Still, the priests obeyed, and the Bible records: "As soon as the feet of the priests who were carrying the Ark touched the water at the river's edge, the water began piling up. . . . Then all the people crossed over" (Josh. 3:15-16, *NLT*).

Although the Jordan soon became a dry riverbed, it was still their *river of liberty*. They were being released into God's promise for them. And though we talk of "Israel" crossing the Jordan in a corporate sense, each Israelite obviously had to cross it individually. It was his or her personal encounter with the *river of liberty*. In the years that followed, each would be able to say "I was there that day!"

A WALK IN THE RIVER

I remember such a day. Pastor Jack Hayford stepped into the *river of liberty* and led 40,000 pastors and leaders with him. It happened at the Promise Keepers Clergy Conference in Atlanta's Georgia Dome in February 1996.

Jack was assigned the topic—*Guarding Your Heart as a Man of Worship*. Early in his brief message Hayford said, "Ultimately everything about my ministry, about my family, about my congregation—everything about my life boils down to my private worship-walk with God."[4]

Hayford suggested that even though these thousands of pastors had gathered in an obvious corporate setting, he hoped that God would somehow insulate each one in his own "booth of private worship" before God's throne.

Jack's brief message dealt primarily with King David, who authored more worship passages in Scripture than any other person and is best remembered by his biblical label, a man after God's own heart (see 1 Sam. 13:14; Acts 13:22).

Hayford particularly drew attention to the fact that David's main priority as Israel's king was to bring the Ark of the Covenant, God's dwelling place, back to Jerusalem. The Ark had been held in captivity for years, and David desired to bring it home.

When he did, as Hayford emphasized, David did not build an elaborate temple for the Ark, but he erected a simple tent, a place called the Tabernacle of David (see Amos 9:11; Acts 15:16-17). David did this, Hayford suggested, because the king wanted the presence of God where he could access it personally and regularly.

When the Ark finally arrived at this tent, David was overwhelmed with joy and danced wildly before God. He even removed his regal garments, perhaps because it was easier to dance freely in his lighter linen undergarments (see 2 Sam. 6:12-15). Of course, to people of that day, it was somewhat like dancing in one's underwear!

David obviously did not do this in a shameful way, Hayford emphasized, but the act clearly angered David's wife, Michal (see 2 Sam. 6:20). But Michal's sharp criticism of David's extravagant worship carried a severe price tag. The text adds this tragic epitaph, "Michal daughter of Saul had no children to the day of her death" (2 Sam. 6:23).

A Hop and Step

Jack Hayford's lesson that day was poignant—but the real message came in the last few minutes when he told about a trip he had taken several years earlier to a nation he did not name. Believers there had an unusual worship tradition that troubled him. Jack explained that as these worshipers would sing bright, happy songs, they would do "something like this—a little hop and step," he said, while adding a quick demonstration.

Jack had seen various worship styles over the years as he traveled, and he certainly understood that some cultures like those in Africa and the Pacific customarily include dancing as a part of their traditions. But this bothered him. He was in a more conservative, western culture. He even spoke to some of the Christian leaders there expressing his dismay, but he did it graciously. He thought he was giving them a point of wisdom. But, as Jack added, "They kindly tolerated my remarks, and didn't rebuke me, but they didn't change their worship either."

When Jack returned home, several of his staff asked about the trip. Some especially wondered about how believers worshiped there. So, in a staff meeting, Hayford gave them a brief demonstration, hopping and stepping with a quick kick or two. He even added a smirk as if to suggest, "Can you believe sane Christians actually do something like this during Sunday morning worship?"

Jack thought little about this "staff dance lesson" until three months later while in a personal time of worship. It had been a deeply moving time and Jack found himself saying, "Jesus, I love you so much, I praise you Lord—I love You more than words can express!"

God's presence filled the room. Suddenly Jack heard God's unmistakable voice, "Will you dance for me?"

DANCING WITH DELIGHT

Jack was stunned. "Everything within me wanted to scream, 'You've got to be kidding!'" he told the 40,000 clergymen. He added, "Never in the world would I do that. I don't do that stuff!"

Yet Jack knew it was an invitation from the Lord Himself to come even closer into His presence. Jack continued, "The option was mine. While I knew I wouldn't lose my salvation or my ministry if I didn't do it, I knew I would lose something of my availability to be intimate with God if I didn't dance."

Jack added, "For a second I thought, *I know what I'll tell the Lord, I'll tell Him I don't know any dance steps.*"

But the Holy Spirit was one jump ahead and said, "You showed all your staff what you saw in that other country. So you know at least one!"

In that private moment Jack began to weep. He saw himself not as a pastor of a large respected congregation but as a two-year-old wearing a diaper and lacking any dance coordination.

Now these many years later, he was recounting this occasion before 40,000 fellow pastors.

What happened next was not unlike Grandma's surprise during that Bible study in northern Thailand. A *river of liberty* had begun to flow in the Georgia Dome, and Jack Hayford was leading the way into it.

Continuing his testimony, Jack explained, "That day in worship I saw that little diaper-clad baby as myself, dancing with delight. And I suddenly felt the shame of my reserve, my pride. It wasn't worth a dime, and I knew I was more interested in saying, 'Lord, I want to know your heart like David. I will not be a Michal who becomes barren.'"

Referring once again to his personal worship experience years earlier, Jack tearfully told the gathering, "In that moment, alone, I started to dance, just like this . . . ," and suddenly this respected leader was more than demonstrating, he was worshiping. Jack Hayford was dancing before the Lord—and in front of 40,000 fellow pastors.

The Georgia Dome exploded into a chorus of weeping and worship. But the weeping was not that of sorrow but of a personal longing for the same liberty that Jack demonstrated. And the worship was not that of a weary liturgical exercise but of a wonderfully ecstatic and expressive encounter with the King!

All of this happened in less than a minute or two, but that *river of liberty* flowed freely for the remainder of the conference. Five years later a well-known pastor of a conservative tradition told me those moments were the most liberating of his entire ministry. Like 40,000 others that day, including myself, Jack Hayford had stepped into God's *river of liberty* and discovered *the personal dimension of intercessory worship*. It is a river of God's delight ready to carry us a new way to a new day in Him. The river is waiting. Just take a few steps!

A FRAGRANT FLAME

RIVER OF HUMILITY:
THE PURIFYING DIMENSION
OF INTERCESSORY WORSHIP

I tossed a match into our fireplace and watched the dry kindling ignite beneath the split oak logs. What would happen that morning in our living room would release an aroma of worship into the heavenlies unlike any I could recall.

That day many things would come together in my mind about the nature of God, what most gives Him delight and the relationship between humility and healing.

This book is about rivers of delight. I have suggested that the flow of prophetic worship ultimately will bring healing to the nations. It will be instrumental in releasing these rivers of God's presence to bring healing to all levels of society. At the heart of this healing will be a spirit of humility.

NO OTHER CHANNEL

Naturally a river that flows from the heart of God, because of its source, will contain something of the very heart of God. Further, if that river is to carry healing in its waters, it will flow through God's people into a dying world. God has chosen no other channel.

The river God showed me before our fireplace that day was a *river of humility*, and it introduces us to *the purifying dimension of intercessory worship*.

It may seem strange to link humility with the healing of nations, but there is a biblical case to be made. God is a humble, holy God. We know God is holy, perfect and complete in every way. The biblical expressions for "holiness" suggest that which is "above weakness and imperfection."[1] Holiness in reference to God connotes separation from all that is human or earthly. God neither needs nor requires anything—or anybody—to sustain Him; He is complete in the unity of His trinity. He is above all that is human.

Yet God created man in a remarkable act of humility. He did it so that we might someday know Him and all His splendor. In creating humankind, God literally gave away a part of Himself. He is above all that is human.

And think of the incarnation—God chose to become a man, in Christ, to live and die among men.

John makes it clear that from the very beginning Christ, as the Word, existed as One *with* God. We read, "In the beginning was the Word, and the Word was with God, and the Word was God" (John 1:1). The "incarnation," a theological expression describing God coming in Christ to live in the world, is described in John's declaration, "The Word became flesh and made his dwelling among us" (John 1:14).

The apostle Paul likewise highlighted the quality of humility in reference to Christ:

Who, being in very nature God . . . made himself nothing, taking the very nature of a servant, being made in human likeness. And being found in appearance as a man, he humbled himself and became obedient to death—even death on a cross! (Phil. 2:6-8).

The river of God's healing power begins in Christ, and Christ is the embodiment of humility.

HUMILITY AND HEALING

The link between humility and healing is seen in God's directive to Solomon, often quoted in the context of revival: "Then if my people who are called by my name will humble themselves and pray and seek my face and turn from their wicked ways, I will hear from heaven and will forgive their sins and heal their land" (2 Chron. 7:14, *NLT*).

The first necessity of this conditional promise is humility. All else flows from that first quality. Then the final promise is that God will "hear from heaven" and "heal their land." Healing the land begins with the humbling of the saints—God's people. What starts with humility ends with healing.

Few people Dee and I have met carry the burden of 2 Chronicles 7:14 more than our friend Nancy Leigh

DeMoss. Nancy, a gifted speaker and writer, who for years has served in a key leadership position with Life Action Ministries and now hosts a daily radio program called *Revive Our Hearts*, aired on more than 300 stations.

Dee and I first got to know Nancy through her challenging teaching on "The Heart That God Revives," which includes a checklist to help believers evaluate their hearts before God. Nancy taught this to 5,000 Campus Crusade for Christ field staff in Fort Collins, Colorado, in 1995, and the result was many hours of public repentance. We sent this teaching by audiocassette to leaders in more than 100 nations who are associated with Every Home for Christ.

Sensing a unique touch on her life, I began praying for Nancy daily. I asked if she had any personal things we might pray about, and she began sending us her prayer letter and itinerary.

In one letter Nancy requested prayer for two specific personal issues. One was for spiritual discernment and the other for protection against pride. Nancy referred to a file of letters of commendation to her from leaders, a file that was getting "quite fat." She explained that although she appreciated the letters, she did not want them to become a catalyst for pride in her life.

Sitting in my prayer closet, I presented Nancy's letter to the Lord. I dismissed her concern about pride because of all the people Dee and I had met in leadership, Nancy seemed least concerned about herself. Still, I prayed.

I concentrated my prayer on Nancy's specific request for spiritual discernment. I felt compelled to write Nancy, even while still in the prayer closet. I grabbed a tablet and began writing.

A SYMBOLIC SUGGESTION

I scribbled a letter, including a quote I had heard once about hearing God's voice. When I finished, I remembered the file of letters Nancy had mentioned, so I added a postscript. But I felt awkward writing it, so I decided to ask Dee if she thought it appropriate.

The postscript suggested that if Nancy had a fireplace, she might want to do something symbolic with some of the letters in her file. Because the Bible tells us all of our works will someday be tested by fire, I suggested that she might consider burning a few of those letters to give her a sense of release. I realized as I wrote it that it was an odd suggestion.

Dee read the postscript and suggested that if I felt God truly had put this on my heart, I should say it. My letter was sent the next day with the postscript included.

Several months later a "Revive Our Hearts" conference was scheduled in our city. Nancy Leigh and Henry Blackaby were to speak. I wrote to Nancy and invited her to our home either for dinner or at least for a time of prayer. Before Nancy could respond, Dee and I left for Australia. We would arrive back home only a few days before the conference began.

While in Australia I phoned my secretary, Debbie Lord, to check in. Debbie told me, "Nancy wrote and said she would be delighted to come to your home for prayer but she had a strange question. She asked if you have a fireplace." Debbie was confused about the request for a fireplace, but I knew immediately what Nancy meant. I told Debbie I would explain it all when we returned and to let Nancy know we did, indeed, have a fireplace.

AN ISAAC MOMENT

The flames grew brighter in our fireplace that chilly March morning as Nancy sat in our living room clutching her file of letters. With her was a longtime personal intercessor whom Nancy wanted to join her during this personal moment.

I had not really talked to Nancy except briefly to confirm this time together in our home. I did not mention the letters because I knew what was on Nancy's mind when she had asked if we had a fireplace. Still it was an awkward moment. I found myself mentally looking for a good "biblical" way out for Nancy, hoping she would not have to do this after all.

Then Abraham's willingness to sacrifice his only son, Isaac, came to mind. "You know, Nancy," I suggested, "it's possible that what's happening today may be one of those Isaac moments."

I recounted the lesson in Genesis 22 when God asks Abraham to sacrifice his only son. It was not until the last moment, as Isaac was placed on an altar stacked with wood and Abraham's hand was clutching the sacrificial blade, that the angel of the Lord shouted, "'Do not hurt the boy in any way, for now I know that you truly fear God'" (Gen. 22:12, *NLT*). In that moment God provided a ram to take Isaac's place.

"Nancy," I advised, "God may have brought you to this point to say, 'Now I know what's in your heart, and you don't need to sacrifice these letters.'"

I quickly added, "Or maybe God wants you to do what I suggested in my letter—sacrifice two or three of these letters as a symbol of your desire to allow nothing to stand between you and God's best."

AN AROMA OF PRAISE

I could tell by the look on her face that Nancy wasn't buying it. *This would be a great time to get out of God's way*, I thought.

Then Nancy spoke. "No, Dick," she said softly. "It has to be all of them, and it has to be today." So after a prayer of release, Nancy stepped toward the fireplace and knelt.

One by one she tossed each letter into the flames. To my amazement, I even saw one of the letters I had written two years earlier tossed into the flames. It must have been the letter in which I told Nancy how her teaching on keeping our hearts pure had so impacted my life and ministry.

Nancy's sacrificial act of worship was pure and prophetic. I believe the smoke of that fire birthed a fragrant aroma of praise that rose to God's very throne. It reminded me of the psalmist's prayer:

> We went through fire and flood. But you brought us to a place of great abundance. That is why I am sacrificing burnt offerings to you—the best of my rams as a pleasing aroma (Ps. 66:12,15, *NLT*).

In the following months a fresh anointing came upon Nancy. Each tape of her teaching or page from one of her books seemed to speak the very heart of God. Nancy had plunged into God's *river of humility*—and she had plunged in all the way. Her experience introduces to us what I call *the purifying dimension of intercessory worship*.

A STRANGE APPREHENSION

I did not realize at the time how deeply that fireplace encounter had impacted my life. If a prophetic word is to "speak before" a person or group in delivering a special message from the Lord, then a prophetic act would be to "act before" a person or group through which a message or directive from God is delivered. Nancy's act of humility spoke a word from God's heart profoundly into mine, and I hope it has the same effect on yours!

By the fall of that year, our executive ministry team had started to draft a 10-year plan for the first decade of the new millennium, called *Completing the Commission*. The plan includes forming strategic alliances to mobilize Christ's Body to launch and sustain systematic, home-by-home evangelism campaigns in every nation by 2010.

The plan was unusually ambitious. Not only would it cost $250 million, but it also had the challenge of reaching restricted-access nations in Arab lands and in remote

African and Asian tribes, plus 335 million homes in China.

By late fall I had decided to set aside December 1998 exclusively for prayer. I knew our senior executive team would understand and even join me for some of the days. As I did during the first time I set aside a month for prayer, December 1987, I committed to spend the hours I would normally spend at my desk or in meetings in prayer.

There was, however, one glitch—many months earlier Dee and I had planned to conduct a *Change the World School of Prayer* in Singapore the first week of December. I decided that since this seminar only involved a few evenings and a Saturday morning, I could spend all the rest of the days of that week and month in prayer, thus honoring my commitment.

As the month approached, I became apprehensive. It was as if God had something significant He wanted me to focus on, but it escaped me.

Suddenly, it was the night before we were to fly to Singapore, and Dee and I were packing. I was in the kitchen when I saw a brown, padded envelope from that day's mail. It was a package from Nancy Leigh.

In the package was a small book by Andrew Murray titled *Humility*. I knew the author well. In fact, our *Change the World School of Prayer* that God has used to train many thousands of believers globally got its name from Andrew Murray's classic book *With Christ in the School of Prayer*.

On the inside cover, Nancy had written a note suggesting the book might be a blessing to me at that season in my life. *Take this with you on your trip*, I thought. I soon discovered that this decision would transform the month.

A THOUGHT IN THE GARDEN

We arrived in Singapore at midnight on Sunday, November 29, and spent the next day adjusting to the time change. Tuesday, December 1, would begin my month of prayer. I decided to go to the botanical gardens to spend my first day in prayer.

Preparing to leave the hotel room, I saw Andrew Murray's book on the hotel coffee table and decided to take it with me. Soon I was sitting on an old wooden bench under a huge banyan tree where I had sat in prayerful worship on several previous trips to Singapore.

As I worshiped quietly, I realized these were the first moments of an entire month committed to seeking the Lord—specifically regarding our emerging 10-year ministry plan. But I felt something was missing.

I grabbed Andrew Murray's little book. For several seconds I gazed at the title—*Humility*. I wondered how this book and its theme might relate to reaching the nations for Jesus. I whispered, "Lord, does this have something to do with my month of prayer?"

AN INFALLIBLE TOUCHSTONE

For some reason, I opened the book not to the beginning but to the last two pages, where I found a brief epilogue by the author. It was titled simply, *A Prayer for Humility*. Sensing it had something to do with my month of prayer, I read:

> Here I will give you an infallible touchstone. It is this; retire from the world and all conversation, only for one month. Neither write, nor read, nor debate anything with yourself. Stop all the former workings of your heart and mind. And, with all the strength of your heart, stand all this month, as continually as you can, in the following form of prayer to God. Offer it frequently on your knees. But whether sitting, walking, or standing, be always inwardly longing and earnestly praying this one prayer to God: "That of His greatness He would make

known to you, and take from your heart, every kind and form and degree of pride, whether it be from evil spirits, or your own corrupt nature; and that He would awaken in you the deepest depth and truth of that humility which can make you capable of His light and Holy Spirit."[2]

That moment I knew I had my prayer theme for the month. Here I was, the first day of a month committed to prayer, while asking God if He had a special focus for the month, and I opened to a page in a book written a hundred years earlier suggesting the reader set aside a month to pray over one theme—*humility*. God had my attention, and He was ready to point me in the direction of His *river of humility*.

> God's glory, and His glory alone, must be our primary desire.

So rich were the insights on humility from Andrew Murray's pen that since those memorable moments I have catalogued several specific focuses to help us soak in this special river of God's delight.

The Essence of Humility

First, there is the *essence* of humility. Essence refers to the fundamental nature or inherent characteristics of an idea or person. It really represents the core or heart of a value. Of course, the heart of humility is God, Himself. Andrew Murray wrote, "The Christian life has suffered loss, because believers have not been distinctly guided to see that nothing is more natural and beautiful and blessed than to be nothing, so that God may be all."[3] Later Murray expressed, "Humility is simply the sense of entire nothingness, which comes when we see how truly God is all, and in which we make way for God to be all."[4]

God's glory, and His glory alone, must be our primary desire. *Humility is key to bringing true glory to God.* Murray wrote:

> Nothing can cure you of the desire to receive honor from men, or of the sensitivity and pain and anger which comes when it is not given, except giving yourself to seek only the glory that comes from God. You will find that the deeper you sink in humility before Him, the nearer He is to fulfill every desire of your faith.[5]

The Excellence of Humility

Second, there is the *excellence* of humility. Excellence concerns the best there is. Excellence generally suggests superiority or preeminence. Andrew Murray believed excellence in Christ is measured by one's humility. He declared, "The life God bestows is imparted not once for all, but each moment continuously, by the unceasing operation of His mighty power. Humility, the place of entire dependence on God, is, from the very nature of things, the first duty and the highest virtue of man. It is the root of every virtue."[6] Murray adds, "Humility is one of the chief and highest of graces. It is one of the most difficult to attain, and one to which our first and greatest efforts ought to be directed."[7]

The Example of Humility

Third, there is the *Example* of humility. I intentionally capitalize the letter *E* in "Example" because I refer not to an abstract quality but to a Person. That Person is Christ. *Jesus is the embodiment of humility*. Andrew Murray summarized, "Christ is the humility of God embodied in human nature."[8]

Andrew Murray was convinced that all Christ did to bring redemption to humanity was because of His humility. Note this even more complete statement from the author:

> It is of inconceivable importance that we should have a correct understanding of who Christ is. We should properly comprehend what really constitutes Him, the Christ, and especially of what may be counted as His chief characteristic—the root and essence of all His character as our Redeemer. There can be only one answer: it is His humility. What is the incarnation but His heavenly humility, His emptying Himself and becoming man? What is His life on earth but humility, His taking the form of a servant? And what is His atonement but humility? "He humbled himself and became obedient unto death."[9]

The Effect of Humility

Fourth, there is the *effect* of humility. Andrew Murray was convinced that all spiritual fruit originated from the soil of humility. He wrote:

> Humility is the only soil in which the graces root; the lack of humility is the sufficient explanation of

every defect and failure. Humility is not so much a grace or virtue along with others; it is the root of all, because it alone assumes the right attitude before God and allows him as God to do all.[10]

Murray expounded on this thought:

If humility is the root of the tree, its nature must be seen in every branch, leaf, and fruit. If humility is the first, the all-inclusive grace of the life of Jesus, the secret of his atonement—then the health and strength of our spiritual life will entirely depend upon our putting this grace first, too.[11]

The Evidence of Humility

Finally, there is the *evidence* of humility. "Evidence" is the proof or validity of a thing that may be in question. When Andrew Murray wrote his book on humility, an emphasis on holiness was sweeping the globe. But Murray was troubled by the potential for pride that easily found entrance to those convinced they had attained holiness. He preached, "Let all teachers of holiness, whether in the pulpit or on the platform, and all seekers after holiness, whether in the closet or in the convention, take warning.

There is no pride so dangerous, none so subtle and insidious, as the pride of holiness."[12]

Andrew Murray pointed to Christ as our supreme example of both holiness and humility: "Jesus the holy One is the humble One. The holiest will always be the humblest. There is none holy but God. We have as much of holiness as we have of God."[13]

> God experiences joy when His children humble themselves before Him and others.

The evidence of our holiness, then, is first seen in our humility before God. Then, our humility before God must be matched by our humility before men. Andrew Murray observes, "It is easy to think we humble ourselves before God. Yet, humility toward man will be the only sufficient proof that our humility before God is real."[14] Murray concludes, "Humility is the very essence of holiness and blessedness. It is the displacement of self by the enthronement of God. Where God is all, self is nothing."[15]

THE AROMA LINGERS

The aroma from our fireplace that March morning lingers

in my memory. There was something purifying about the flow of God's presence that day. It was a river of delight, and the delight was in the joy God experiences when His children humble themselves before Him—and others.

That day I realized that those whose ministries and strategies will most impact the world for Jesus will be those who most humble themselves before God. I knew Every Home for Christ had to pursue our 10-year ministry plan from a foundation of humility if we were to succeed. The alliances and partnerships needed to complete the Great Commission will necessitate a unity that will only come through a new level of humility.

Andrew Murray was right in his assumption. Humility is the infallible touchstone that will make all this possible. Intercessory worship plays such a critical role in this humility because, as the late Paul E. Billheimer said so persuasively, "Here is the greatest value of praise: it decentralizes self. The worship and praise of God demands a shift of center from self to God."[16] God-saturated intercession (which defines intercessory worship) focuses first on God through praise and then on others, which is intercession.

Nothing I know of has a greater capacity to unite Christ's Body in purity and humility than a passionate movement of intercessory worship. And as this unity through humility emerges, I believe it will release something of a flow of prophetic purity that will "speak before" the whole world declaring the transforming power of Christ's love. What a glorious river to swim in!

A FIGHT OF DELIGHT

RIVER OF RECOVERY: THE PERSUASIVE DIMENSION OF INTERCESSORY WORSHIP

My heart pounded as I sped home along a Los Angeles freeway. Dee had just phoned telling me to come home quickly. Our daughter, Ginger, had a fever of almost 105. Our precious six-year-old had caught a virus a few days earlier, but we had paid little attention—until now.

When I arrived a half hour later, Dee was waiting at the door. She handed me a piece of paper.

"The doctor just called this prescription in to the pharmacy," she said. "If Ginger doesn't improve soon, we'll have to take her to the hospital."

> A spark of special faith touched my heart the moment I said the words, "I really need to pray."

As I turned to head out the door, I hesitated. Something bothered me. I had not prayed for Ginger. I turned to Dee and said, "I really need to pray for Ginger first, and then I'll get the prescription."

DELIGHTING IN SONG

Neither Dee nor I considered it a lack of faith to go to a doctor, but we also knew God could heal and restore. In that instant as I went to go pray for Ginger, a spark of special faith touched my heart. It came the moment I said the words, "I really need to pray."

However, that faith was tested when I sat on Ginger's bed and touched her burning skin. Her eyes were half open and her face pale. I had a fleeting thought that my prayer would not accomplish much. But suddenly I remembered that if anyone delights in the Lord, "he will give you the desires of your heart" (Ps. 37:4).

I realized I was not called merely to pray at that moment but to delight in the Lord. I looked into her tired eyes and said, "Ginger, I'm not going to pray for you today." Before I could say more, Ginger frowned. She had always counted on Dad's prayers. But I quickly added, "Ginger, I've decided not to pray for you—instead I'm going to sing over you."

Her discouraged look became one of puzzlement. I explained, "Ginger, in the Bible there's a story about a battle God's people had against a much stronger army than their own. When they asked God what to do, He just said, 'Sing songs of praise to Me as you face the battlefield. If you do that, I will come and fight this battle for you.' So they sang and God helped them win the battle" (see 2 Chron. 20).

I further explained, "There's also a Scripture in the psalms where God says that if we delight in Him, He will give us the desires of our hearts (see Ps. 20:4). He knows that your desire is to get well. So I'm going to sing a song over you that delights in God."

MONITORING A MIRACLE

My simple song told God I loved Him and delighted in His presence. Soon I felt a strange sensation. Sweat from Ginger's forehead poured down like a torrent. Her fever had broken that instant! By evening, her temperature was normal. The battle had not been won in praying but in delighting. And I never bought that description!

Two years later I shared my "fight of delight" experience on *The 700 Club* television program. Unbeknownst to me, a family in California had gathered around an ailing father's bedside just after that program was aired. The testimony of what happened that day came to me from one of our secretaries who knew the family.

That morning the wife of the ill man had seen the program and heard the brief story of the miracle of my song. She decided to do the same thing over her husband.

The family gathered around the man and began singing. Within moments, his heartbeat and blood pressure became normal! The hospital monitors recorded the story. His elevated temperature went down in minutes. Soon everyone was in tears, nurses included. They had been monitoring a miracle. The man was released soon after.

RETURNING TO NORMAL

These experiences of spontaneous song help us understand *the persuasive dimension* of *prophetic intercessory worship*. We see this dimension often in Scripture, and it is usually linked to the power of music. In these cases melodic worship releases a flow of God's presence that might be defined as a *river of recovery*. Recovery means renewing, reviving or returning to normal.

Several Scripture passages describe the persuasive power of music—each involving a harp or other musical instruments. Most familiar is the account of young David who plays his harp over the deranged King Saul. The Bible says, "And whenever the tormenting spirit from God troubled Saul, David would play the harp. Then Saul would feel better, and the tormenting spirit would go away" (1 Sam. 16:23, *NLT*). Earlier the passage says, "Now the Spirit of the LORD had left Saul, and the LORD sent a tormenting spirit that filled him with depression and fear" (v. 14, *NLT*).

Interestingly, several servants also realized this soothing power of music. They suggested a remedy to the king, "Let us find a good musician to play the harp for you whenever the tormenting spirit is bothering you. The harp music will quiet you, and you will soon be well again" (v. 16, *NLT*). It worked. David was summoned, and when he played his harp, "Saul would feel better, and the tormenting spirit would go away" (v. 23, *NLT*).

A HARP AND A PROPHET

The war between Israel and Moab in 2 Kings 3:1-11 provides another biblical example. King Joram of Israel, King Jehoshaphat of Judah and the king of Edom formed an alliance to fight King Mesha of Moab, who had rebelled against Israel. As the three allied armies traveled in the wilderness, they soon found themselves without water. Desperate for divine direction, King Jehoshaphat asks the others, "Is there no prophet of the LORD with us? If there is, we can ask the LORD what to do" (v. 11, *NLT*).

Then it was discovered that Elisha was among them. At this time Elisha was early on in his ministry, and he was still known more as Elijah's former assistant. (By now the old prophet, Elijah, had been dead for some time.)

Still, Jehoshaphat felt confident in Elisha because of his past connection with Elijah, so he encouraged the others, saying, "The LORD will speak through him" (v. 12, *NLT*).

However, when they summoned Elisha and sought his council, the young prophet said emphatically, "I want no part of you" (v. 13, *NLT*).

Eventually Elisha gave in, but he made it clear he was doing so only because of his personal respect for King Jehoshaphat of Judah (see v. 14, *NLT*). And it is at this moment that Elisha makes a peculiar request: "Now bring me someone who can play the harp," (v. 15, *NLT*).

Why a harp? Because "While the harp was being played, the power of the LORD came upon Elisha, and he said, 'This is what the LORD says'" (vv. 15-16, *NLT*). What follows is a prophetic directive from God that promises victory over the Moabites.

Another example of the persuasive power of prophetic worship is seen in Isaiah's prophecy of Israel's fruitful future (see Isa. 30:18-33). Note just some of the promises from this passage:

> Then the LORD will bless you with rain at planting time. There will be wonderful harvests . . . there will be streams of water flowing down every mountain and hill. . . . So it will be when the LORD begins to heal his people and cure the wounds he gave them. . . . *The people of God will sing a song of joy, like the songs at the holy festivals.* . . . And the LORD will make his majestic voice heard. With angry

indignation he will bring down his mighty arm on his enemies. . . . He will strike them down . . . And as the LORD strikes them, *his people will keep time with the music of tambourines and harps* (Isa. 30:23-32, *NLT,* emphasis added).

Again we see an unmistakable link between prophetic melodic worship and God's response. His response includes a release of rivers that heal: "There will be streams of water flowing . . . when the LORD begins to heal his people" (Isa. 30:25-26, *NLT*).

In these examples, melodies are used to soothe, restore and release a prophetic directive from God. These melodies seem to possess power to overcome demonic authorities in the invisible realm.

I would suggest that this *persuasive dimension* of intercessory worship releases a *river of recovery*—a soothing place of restoration and renewal.

A MINOR PROPHET WITH A MAJOR MESSAGE

Perhaps the greatest example of a biblical appeal for restoration and recovery that also comes in the form of a song is sung by the prophet Habakkuk. The prophet's song is found in the third chapter of Habakkuk. Habakkuk may have been a minor prophet, but he brings to us a major message. Various translations begin chapter three by noting the Hebrew expression *shigionoth*, which appears in the Hebrew text. For example, the *New International Version* begins: "A prayer of Habakkuk the prophet. On shigionoth" (Hab. 3:1). Of course, without some sort of explanation this makes little sense. Thus, the *New International Version* includes a footnote stating: "Probably a literary or musical term."

Actually, the word "shigionoth" is a musical instruction, a reference to something sung or accompanied by music.[1] Thus, the *New Living Translation* appropriately begins chapter three: "This prayer was sung by the prophet Habakkuk." Interestingly, at the end of the chapter in that same Bible, we see this concluding parenthetical directive: "(For the choir director: This prayer is to be accompanied by stringed instruments)."

This suggests that chapter three in its entirety is a song. It is a song of restoration and recovery. Habakkuk is appealing to God in song, asking Him to do again what He had once done miraculously for His people. A closer look at the prophet's song reveals at least three primary focuses.

A Song of Anticipation

First, Habakkuk's song is one of *anticipation*. There is a passionate pleading for a visitation from God in the prophet's song. Habakkuk recalls the past when God visited His people and then sings this appeal: "I have heard all about you, LORD, and I am filled with awe by the amazing things you have done. In this time of our deep need, begin again to help us, as you did in years gone by. Show us your power to save us. And in your anger, remember your mercy" (Hab. 3:2, *NLT*).

Habakkuk is appealing, through song, for renewal. "Renewal" is defined as "the act of restoring something to its original condition; to be energized afresh; to be revived, restored and revitalized."[2] It is synonymous with the word "recovery."

A Song of Amazement

Second, the prophet's song is one of *amazement*. Habakkuk sings his vision of an awesome God who is His splendor and power:

> I see God, the Holy One, moving across the deserts. . . . His brilliant splendor fills the heavens, and the earth is filled with his praise! What a

wonderful God he is! Rays of brilliant light flash from his hands. He rejoices in his awesome power. . . . When he looks, the nations tremble. He shatters the everlasting mountains and levels the eternal hills. But his power is not diminished in the least! (Hab. 3:3-6, *NLT*).

Our songs of intercessory worship, if they are to persuade invisible powers, need to be filled with the awe and wonder of God's splendor and majesty as was Habakkuk's song.

We need more amazement in our worship. These words of Habakkuk provide an excellent model. Such worship also can become uniquely prophetic, even without our awareness, as we declare God's greatness "before" or "in front of" thrones, powers, rulers and authorities in the unseen realm (see Eph. 3:10; 6:12; Col. 1:15-16). Intercessory worship carries this amazement into the heavenlies and reminds these rulers and authorities that the same power that shatters the everlasting mountains will shatter their thrones!

A Song of Assurance

Finally, Habakkuk's song is one of *assurance*. There's a quiet confidence and certainty in the concluding words of the prophet's song. He sings:

Even though the fig trees have no blossoms, and there are no grapes on the vine; even though the olive crop fails, and the fields lie empty and barren; even though the flocks die in the fields, and the cattle barns are empty, yet I will rejoice in the LORD! I will be joyful in the God of my salvation. The Sovereign LORD is my strength! He will make me as surefooted as a deer and bring me safely over the mountains (Hab. 3:17-19, *NLT*).

Look again at Habakkuk's interesting concluding note: "(For the choir director: This prayer is to be accompanied by stringed instruments)" (Hab. 3:19, *NLT*). Habakkuk understood *the persuasive dimension of intercessory worship*. He saw the soothing power of a melody. And his song embodied elements of both intercession and worship. He pleaded in song on behalf of God's people (intercession), while in the same song he exalted God for His awe and splendor (worship). And as he sang, harps (stringed instruments) were helping him release God's *river of recovery*.

We, too, should fill our worship with songs of anticipation, amazement and assurance. Try singing Habakkuk chapter three instead of just reading it. Many psalms also can be sung spontaneously in the same way. So don't hold back. Make up your own songs. There are, indeed, rivers of delight beckoning us to bathe in God's soothing pools of recovery. They are as close as your closet of prayer. Take the plunge!

A WIG AND A HARLEY

RIVER OF GENEROSITY: THE PASSIONATE DIMENSION OF INTERCESSORY WORSHIP

The Texas pastor trembled as he stepped from behind the pulpit and descended the carpeted stairs. Standing level with his congregation, he was about to do the unthinkable. It was time to reveal his long-kept secret.

Pastor Kenneth Phillips of Austin, Texas, had been fasting for seven days, pleading with God for a release of

His presence as recorded in the book of Acts. During his fast, Kenneth had meditated over Acts 3–4, where a lame man was dramatically healed and a whole city turned upside down (see Acts 3:1-9; 4:1-4,16). He read repeatedly how Jewish leaders referred to this healing as "a notable miracle" that could not be refuted (Acts 4:16, *NKJV*). That notable miracle resulted in 5,000 conversions in a single day (see Acts 4:4).

As Kenneth's fast was ending, the veteran pastor pleaded again with God, asking what it would take to see at least one notable miracle in our day that could so impact a city.

In that instant, Kenneth heard God's unmistakable voice: "Step up. Come up here!" Pastor Phillips realized God was inviting him to come higher in Himself, as well as calling him to step into a whole new dimension of death to self in his Christian walk.

A WIG AND A WILLING HEART

Convinced every hindrance in his life had to go, Kenneth thought immediately of his hairpiece. Most parishioners had no idea their pastor wore a toupee. Even barbers thought the toupee to be Pastor Phillips's real hair.

Now Kenneth Phillips felt he needed to lay his toupee aside as a sacrifice, indicating his desire to see more of God's glory. Kenneth knew what he had to do—and it had to be done that very Sunday—before the entire congregation.

As Pastor Phillips concluded his Sunday message "One Notable Miracle" (appropriately titled), he walked down from behind the pulpit and stood trembling before his congregation. His voice breaking, the senior pastor told his congregation he was more desperate than ever for God's presence and was ready to remove any hindrance that might stand in the way.

To a stunned gathering, Kenneth Phillips explained his secret and, in an instant, removed his hairpiece and abruptly laid it before the altar.[1] In that moment, God's glory flowed over the congregation. People fell to their knees and faces, weeping. The revival the pastor had so desperately sought came. All it took was a wig and a willing heart. His sacrifice became a prophetic act, which revealed *the passionate dimension of intercessory worship*.

This pastor's sacrifice was an act "before the people" that touched hearts with a passion for God. It was an act of intercessory worship, because it not only involved a sacrifice of worship, but it also was the pastor's final act of

God-saturated intercession that released his long-sought plea—revival!

When Pastor Phillips sacrificed the security of his toupee, he stepped into a *river of generosity,* releasing a flow of blessing to others. When generosity is released into others' needs, it becomes intercessory. If such an act also involves the prophetic, as Pastor Phillips's act did, it becomes an act of prophetic intercessory worship.

TRIPPING ON A MIRACLE

Many mentors motivate us toward spiritual maturity. I especially remember a young pastor named Doug Ramsey who came to serve our church in southern Wisconsin when I was a teen. Pastor Doug helped me through some tough times, ultimately steering me toward Bible college.

I was fascinated by Pastor Ramsey's constant joy and the unique ways God blessed him. Our church did not pay much, but Pastor had a keen business sense. If there were some good deals to be made, Pastor Doug would find them. He was also a private contractor who had built his own home, saving him thousands of dollars.

Pastor built his house on prime land along the river. I heard him tell my father, a church deacon, the miracle of how he bought the property for "practically nothing."

One day as Pastor Ramsey was driving along the river, he saw the beautiful lot surrounded by expensive houses. He felt led to "claim" the property in prayer, though it was unlikely he could afford it. Further, no For Sale sign was posted. Still, he could imagine his house on that very land. Doug stopped his car and walked out into the deep weeds and asked God to open a way for him to acquire the property. Pastor Ramsey often prayed bold prayers of faith like this.

Doug Ramsey told my dad that as he walked back to his car, he tripped over something in the weeds. It was a fallen For Sale sign that appeared to have been there for years. It listed the blurred phone number of a private owner living 90 miles away.

Later that day Doug Ramsey called the owner, an elderly man who seemed shocked that someone had called him about the lot. It had been for sale for years without a single offer. Apparently, the eccentric man had never checked on his For Sale sign. Pastor asked the man how much he wanted for the land. The owner responded, "What will you give me?"

Doug offered an amount so low it embarrassed him, but the man only said, "Sold!" It was another blessing for Doug. In the weeds, he had tripped over a miracle.

A DARK AND DISTANT PLACE

That was how everything happened to Doug Ramsey. He was always blessed.

One day, before leaving for Bible college, I asked Pastor why some people seemed especially blessed though we all serve the same God? It had all begun, he explained, when he was a 19-year-old in Bible college. He had a dream of owning a Harley Davidson motorcycle. He calculated that if he worked all through the summer, spending 16 hours a day in the Iowa cornfields, he would have enough to buy a motorcycle by September.

By summer's end Doug had saved enough to fulfill his dream. Before heading back to college, he bought the Harley. Doug looked forward to the next day when he would take his new bike to church so everyone could see it.

Doug was up early that Sunday, and he arrived at the church before the service started. He parked his new bike by the front door. Standing close to his Harley he greeted people. Everybody was complimentary. He was noticeably proud.

Doug looked forward to the pastor's sermon but soon learned their church had a special guest that morning—a missionary from Africa. Doug listened as the veteran missionary spoke. He described the challenges of working in Africa, where in many places the roads are rough and sometimes nonexistent. Yet his greatest need was for a new vehicle to replace his broken-down Jeep.

A HARLEY HARVEST

Doug wept as the pastor closed the service. His pastor explained that he believed they should help this missionary with the cost of new transportation. The pastor then asked people to pray about what they might give. Something began to stir in Doug's heart. He knew he should give something, but he had just spent all he had on his Harley.

The pastor explained that they would take a special offering for their guest.

Doug knew he had nothing to give. Then he felt God speak, "You do have something you can give, and you should give it now."

Doug Ramsey stood in his pew and stepped into the aisle. His tears flowed freely. He headed for the parking lot. What happened next brought many tears to the congregation that morning. The front door opened again, and down the aisle came Doug Ramsey, pushing his shiny new Harley toward the altar.

The missionary, too, wept as Doug said through tears, "I know this isn't a Jeep, but I want you to have my Harley to help reach lost souls in Africa."

Now, all these years later, Doug Ramsey was telling me that from the moment he sacrificed his Harley, he could not keep up with all of God's blessings.

Hearing Doug Ramsey's story I thought, *I bet there's a Harley harvest happening somewhere in Africa right now because of Pastor's sacrifice.* I wondered how many remote places that Harley had gone in helping the missionary take the gospel to those who had never heard the good news.

> When we give unto the Lord with a pure heart, generosity becomes one of the most tangible acts of worship possible.

THE DELIGHT OF GIVING

As with Pastor Phillips's toupee, Doug Ramsey's Harley offering was an act of intercessory worship that led him into God's *river of generosity*. These sacrifices gave joy and honor to God. Such sacrificial giving flows from passion.

This deep Christ-saturated zeal leads to passionate acts that may have profound and prophetic implications. The wig and the Harley make this clear. Both were acts of sacrificial worship.

Sadly, giving is often overlooked as an act of worship. Yet when we give unto the Lord with a pure heart, generosity becomes one of the most tangible acts of worship possible. To enter God's *river of generosity* is to discover the delight of giving.

How we handle our money says much about our maturity as believers. Handling finances is a recurring theme in Scripture. Often God's blessings are directly linked to our giving.

Regarding generosity that touched a poor man, Moses told God's people, "Give generously to him and do so without a grudging heart; then because of this the Lord your God will bless you in all your work and in everything you put your hand to" (Deut. 15:10). Giving to others is an act that both worships as well as honors God.

MISSING THE MESSAGE

Hetty Green, a nineteenth-century millionaire from Massachusetts, clearly missed this message. Hetty had inherited a small fortune in 1835. Through shrewd management, she grew the fortune to over $100 million and became known as "The Wizard of Wall Street."

Yet Hetty lived like a pauper. When her young son Edward broke his leg, Hetty took him to a charity hospital, appearing as a beggar. Edward was not treated properly, thus his leg was amputated. In her later years, Hetty Green lived in a tenement house, usually subsisting on a diet of cold eggs and onions. She wanted to save even the cost of heating her food. She wore newspapers for underwear and allowed only the lower half of her petticoat to be laundered. At her death in 1916, Hetty Green left $125 million to her heirs. Yet money had made her miserable.[2]

Imagine if Hetty had developed the gift of giving! When Paul provided believers at Rome a list of important objectives for mature spiritual growth, he specifically mentioned giving.

Paul wrote, "Just as our bodies have many parts and each part has a special function, so it is with Christ's body. We are all parts of his one body, and each of us has different work to do. And since we are all one body in Christ, we belong to each other, and each of us needs all the others" (Rom. 12:4-5, *NLT*). The apostle then suggests a variety of gifts we might possess, including the gift of giving (see

vv. 5-10, *NLT*). Paul goes on to write, "If you have money, share it generously" (v. 8, *NLT*).

Paul later refers to this gift as "the grace of giving" (2 Cor. 8:7). He told Corinthian believers, "But just as you excel in everything—in faith, in speech, in knowledge, in complete earnestness and in your love for us—see that you also excel in this grace of giving" (2 Cor. 8:7). Paul's call to excellence in giving is likewise a call to excellence in worship. We see this theme developed even more substantively in 2 Corinthians 9, in which Paul uses the analogy of a farmer planting seeds to describe our generosity in giving.

PRINCIPLES FOR PLANTING

Paul continued his instructions on flowing in God's *river of generosity* as he writes:

> But remember this—if you give little, you will get little. A farmer who plants just a few seeds will get only a small crop, but if he plants much, he will reap much. Every one must make up his own mind as to how much he should give. Don't force anyone to give more than he really wants to, for cheerful givers are the ones God prizes. God is

able to make it up to you by giving you everything you need and more, so that there will not
only be enough for your own needs, but plenty
left over to give joyfully to others. For God, who
gives seed to the farmer to plant, and later on,
good crops to harvest and eat, will give you more
and more seed to plant and will make it grow so
that you can give away more and more fruit from
your harvest (2 Cor. 9:6-8,10, *TLB*).

In this single passage we see five clear principles for planting as we cultivate excellence in this grace and gift called
giving. They include:

Principle #1: Our Harvest Will Be in Proportion to Our Planting

This is obvious from Paul's words, "A farmer who plants
just a few seeds will get only a small crop, but if he plants
much, he will reap much" (v. 6, *TLB*). Sadly, our spiritual
crops are often tragically small because we keep so much
of what comes to us for ourselves instead of releasing it to
others in need. It is like the old country preacher passing
his hat for a visiting evangelist. When he got it back, he
tipped it over, and not even a dime fell out. He prayed, "I

thank thee, O Lord, that in thy marvelous grace, I got my hat back." Those who hold back at planting time will be kept back at harvest time. I'm afraid there are too many empty hats in the Kingdom, and the results will show at harvest time.

Principle #2: Our Planting Will Be in Proportion to Our Sacrifice

Paul writes next, "Every one must make up his own mind as to how much he should give. Don't force anyone to give more than he really wants to" (v. 7, *TLB*). Here we see that giving is a decision. It is also synonymous with planting. Thus, the amount of seed we are able to plant will be in proportion to the sacrifice we are willing to make. Little sacrifice—little seed. Little seed—little harvest.

Principle #3: Our Worship Will Be in Proportion to Our Delight

There is in these thoughts of Paul an element of delighting in God—"Cheerful givers are the ones God prizes" (v. 7, *TLB*). This speaks of delighting in God. Here we find a factor vital to this grace Paul calls giving. *Sacrificial giving is an act of joyful worship.* It brings delight to the heart of God and delighting in God is worship. Further, when our giving intervenes in another person's life it becomes intercessory in nature. For example, a person may give a gift that helps provide someone the gospel who comes to Christ as the result. That is both an act of worship and an act of intercession. This is how our giving becomes intercessory worship.

Principle #4: Our Blessing Will Be in Proportion to God's Ability

The text continues: "God is able to make it up to you by giving you everything you need and more" (v. 8, *TLB*). God's ability to bless, of course, is unlimited. Sacrificial givers are never shortchanged by God.

Principle #5: The Abundance of the Blessing Will Be in Proportion to Our Faith

Paul concludes his teaching on giving with this reminder, "For God . . . will give you more and more seed to plant and will make it grow so that you can give away more and more fruit from your harvest" (v. 10, *TLB*).

Here Paul compares money invested in others to seed that produces additional fruit, eventually producing even more seed. More seed allows us to expand our harvest seasons, reaping yet greater harvests and increasing our abundance of yet additional seed. Thus the *river of generosity* grows deeper and wider!

Most importantly, our true return on investment is the harvest of lost people who come to Christ! Look again at this important command of Christ.

> Do not store up for yourselves treasures on earth, where moth and rust destroy, and where thieves break in and steal. But store up for yourselves treasures in heaven, where moth and rust do not destroy, and where thieves do not break in and steal. For where your treasure is, there your heart will be also (Matt. 6:19-21).

The ultimate return on investment is the harvest. Converted souls represent our only true eternal investment. God's *river of generosity* is thus like an irrigation channel that flows through the nations making this harvest possible.

THE WISE WOODCUTTER

A saintly old man from North Carolina named Frank Case lived out these principles. Frank is possibly the most remarkable giver I have known. He had a passion for the lost that led to extraordinary sacrificial giving. He embodied the concept that giving is an act of intercessory worship.

Frank Case died in 1976 at age 86. That year I joined the staff of World Literature Crusade, now Every Home for Christ. His death was a celebration of "harvest giving" that touched millions of lives.

F. C. Case was not a man of many resources. Even into his 70s, Frank read his Bible by the light of a kerosene lantern. In fact, it was only a few years before his death that Frank finally brought electricity into his cabin.

For many years Frank's diet consisted of pinto beans, and when he could afford it, a ham bone. He once wrote to us explaining that for years a $10 bag of pinto beans would last him an entire month. This, he said, allowed him to give even more to help reach the multitudes for Jesus.

In Frank's later years, he acquired all his income from one source—chopping wood in the Carolina hills and selling it as firewood in nearby towns. He did this even after he turned 80, and he did it without ever owning something as modern as a chainsaw. Several of his monthly checks sent to Every Home for Christ in his final few years exceeded $600. By the time Frank passed away, we calculated that at least 8 million people in nations scattered throughout the world had received the gospel through EHC because of F. C. Case. He lived in God's *river of generosity* and no doubt helped thousands, if not tens of thousands, find Christ.

Understandably, we nicknamed him "the wise woodcutter."

There are, as we have seen, a variety of rivers of delight that flow from the heart of God, but few, I doubt, are any more delightful to our Father than this *river of generosity*. It seems to flow out through His willing children and then directly back to His throne in their worship. Cheerful givers, indeed, are the ones God prizes! To me, F. C. Case sailed into heaven in this *river of generosity*. And I am sure that upon his arrival, he found all of heaven rejoicing. One can almost imagine an angel telling God, "I can explain all the noise. Frank Case has arrived!"

ADAM'S SONG

RIVER OF DESTINY:
THE POSSESSIVE DIMENSION OF
INTERCESSORY WORSHIP

I am not sure I always recognize when an action in prayer (or worship) is prophetic. Nor am I sure it even needs to be recognized as such at the time. Sometimes it may be months or even years before we realize that such an act was, indeed, prophetic.

That's what I believe happened the day Dee and I prayed and sang over Garrett and Carol Lee in the prayer room at Every Home for Christ.

A few days earlier our first grandchild, Jack, had been born. Jack was a great joy, and our EHC staff rejoiced with us. Yet for Garrett and Carol Lee, our joy quickly became a sad reminder of their personal loss. Just days after Jack's birth, Carol had a miscarriage. With it came the fear often associated with a first-baby miscarriage—the fear that maybe one will never have children. Dee and I could see that the Lees were heartbroken.

Garrett and Carol were both on our staff, so it was easy for me as president to invite them to my office and suggest that Dee and I would like to pray with them. Tears came to Carol's eyes the moment I mentioned it.

Moments later we were sitting in our ministry prayer room—a small chapel where we have little flags of all the nations positioned in the molding around the room. In the center is a large, lighted globe. This creates an atmosphere that reminds us we are always "praying among the nations."

But that day, prayer for Garrett and Carol would be particularly personal. Only much later (months, in fact) would these flags have special meaning in the miracle that would follow.

MEMORIES OF A SONG

As we sat in the prayer room, I looked at Garrett and Carol

without a clue as to what to pray. My mind was blank. Dee rescued me by saying that we wanted them to know how much we loved them and that life sometimes surprises us with difficult challenges. Nothing about these challenges, she continued, ever changes the character of God.

As Dee spoke, I had the sudden memory of a song. But it was not a song I had sung; rather, it was a song I had *heard* about someone singing. The song had been sung years earlier to an audience of one, in a church Dee and I had been attending at the time. The soloist was a little eight-year-old girl named Aimee. The audience was our pastor at the time, Jack Hayford. Jack recounts this experience in his inspiring book, *Worship His Majesty.*[1]

Little Aimee had grabbed Jack's coattail one Sunday morning as Pastor headed down a hall between services. She asked happily, "Pastor Jack, wanna hear my song?"

Jack could not resist Aimee's innocence. Even though he was in a hurry, he waited as the child sang her made-up song. It was over in moments, and Pastor assured her it was a great song. Aimee's tune brought back memories for Jack, just as all these years later, I was now recalling his memories.

Aimee's melody reminded Jack of a message he had spoken about nine years earlier at The Church On The

Way in Van Nuys, California, where he pastored. His sermon was titled "The Conceiving and Bearing of Life." It was based on the opening verses of Isaiah 54.

Jack especially highlighted the first words of the passage—"Sing, O barren woman, you who never bore a child"—emphasizing the irony of a prophet in that culture telling a "despairing reject of society" to sing. It seemed foolish to suggest such a thing, at least in ancient Israel. As Hayford explained:

> In ancient Israel, nothing prompted a song less than the barren condition of a woman. A woman without children was disenfranchised, discredited, suspect of spiritual unworthiness and potentially subject to divorce—all on the grounds of her biological incapability for childbearing. Into this depressing situation of personal hopelessness, the prophet commands the woman to sing and, incredibly, directs her to start preparing a nursery, for there are babies (plural) coming![2]

Jack then read the heart of the passage. It is a passage most preachers use to support a new building project or some expansion of ministry. In reality, it speaks of a barren woman having babies and the need to build a bigger place to house them. Jack read, "Enlarge the place of your tent. . . . For you shall expand to the right and to the left, and your descendants will inherit the nations. . . . You will forget the shame of your youth. . . . For your Maker is your husband, the LORD of hosts is His name" (Isa. 54:2-5, *NKJV*).

BARRENNESS IN THE BLEAK SPOTS

Jack explained that his message that morning was not a lesson on having children in a physical sense but on overcoming barrenness in the bleak spots of our Christian walk. Worship, Jack suggested, was a key to bring us to victory when circumstances appear hopelessly unfruitful.

Jack suddenly paused. He was midway through his sermon and sensed the Holy Spirit's prompting. He explained:

> My message [this morning] has specifically *not* had to do with natural childbearing. . . . Still, the Holy Spirit is impressing upon me that there is a couple here this morning who has longed for a child, who has been told they cannot have one and whom the Lord wants to know He is present to speak to your need in a personal way this morning.[3]

What Pastor Jack said next, I believe, was prophetic, and introduces us to *the possessive dimension of intercessory worship*. It is a dimension that releases us into God's *river of destiny* for our lives.

Jack then spoke to whoever felt this "word" was for them: "Begin to fill your house with song, and as you do, the life-giving power of that song will establish a new atmosphere and make way for the conception which you have desired."

Jack did not specifically ask anyone to indicate his or her personal situation. He was merely speaking what he felt God was impressing on him in that moment.

About a year later, Mike and Cheri, a couple in the congregation, were talking with Pastor Hayford about the dedication of their first baby that following Sunday. The Church On The Way had a congregation of thousands, and Jack could not recall ever having had a conversation with the couple. After a few opening comments, Mike said: "Pastor Jack, we wanted to talk with you for a few minutes before Sunday's dedication because there's something about it we felt you would want to know."

Mike recounted the pastor's sermon on bearing life a year earlier, and particularly, the prophetic word.

"That word you spoke, Pastor," Mike explained, "the one about a couple who desperately wanted a child—that was us."

Mike told how he and Cheri went home that day and began filling their house with spiritual songs. He and his wife would walk hand in hand into each room and sing spontaneous praises and worship to the Lord. They were certain that this new, precious baby girl soon to be dedicated was the result of God responding to their songs.

Mike and Cheri named their daughter Aimee, and it would be eight years later that this same little girl would sing her song to Pastor Jack, triggering the memory. And now Jack's memory had become mine, as Dee and I prepared to pray over Garrett and Carol Lee. *I knew I had to sing.*

A SONG OF PROMISE

By the time Dee had shared her feelings, which only took a few minutes, I sensed even more that Carol felt "barren." I again recalled Isaiah's prophecy, "Sing, O barren woman" (Isa. 54:1). I quickly turned to the passage and read it to Garrett and Carol. I told them I felt I was to sing a song of fruitfulness over Carol.

Before going into the prayer room, a psalm had come to my mind, Psalm 20, which I sensed was particularly for the Lees. However, I had not thought of singing it until then. It is a psalm of hope and encouragement. I asked them to bear with me as I attempted to sing Psalm 20, spontaneously, as a prayer. They knew I was not a soloist.

Singing a psalm in someone's presence was not something I was comfortable doing. In fact, other than the song I had sung over my sick daughter years before, as I mentioned in chapter 8, to this point in my 35 years of ministry I had only done something like this once before, an experience I described in my book *Pathways of Delight*.

So I began to sing, one verse at a time, through Psalm 20. Like little Aimee's song, it was a made-up melody and certainly nothing special. I sang, "May the LORD answer you when you are in distress; may the name of the God of Jacob protect you. May he send you help from the sanctuary and grant you support from Zion" (Ps. 20:1-2).

I continued, "May he give you the desire of your heart and make all your plans succeed. We will shout for joy when you are victorious and will lift up our banners in the name of our God. May the LORD grant all your requests" (vv. 4-5).

I sang each verse slowly, and in my heart faith began to build. Verse seven was especially encouraging, "Some trust in chariots and some in horses, but we trust in the name of the LORD our God."

As I finished my song, faith filled my heart. It felt like the faith of 1 Corinthians 12:9 that comes as a supernatural gift.

"Carol," I suggested, "what I just sang contains a promise—not just a promise from God but a promise to you from us—that when God gives you your heart's desire, we will return to this very place waving banners and shouting joyfully over your victory. We'll even invite the whole staff to join us."

I looked at a calendar as we left the prayer room. It was November 2, 1998.

A FLAG FOR ADAM

In a few weeks (early December) we heard that Carol was again pregnant. Nine months after that, little Adam Lee was born. On September 9, 1999, just three days after his birth, Garrett and Carol brought the tiny infant to the office. We called everyone together and for the first time told them about my song and promise sung over Garrett and Carol barely 10 months earlier.

Knowing that Garrett and Carol were bringing baby Adam to the office that morning, and remembering the promise I had made of coming back to the prayer room—waving banners—I asked my secretary, Debbie Lord, if she would locate some banners for us to wave. Debbie phoned a few nearby churches that she knew displayed banners, but could not reach anyone in time to get permission to borrow even a few.

Then Debbie got an idea, "What about waving the flags that we have in the prayer room?" she asked me. "Flags are banners, aren't they?"

Because all the flags in our prayer room are on pencil-size sticks placed in the molding around the prayer room, they could easily be removed. So, we had our banners.

I told the staff the whole story, including my promise that when Garrett and Carol experienced their miracle, Dee and I would return, inviting the staff to join us, waving banners and shouting for joy. So I invited all who wished to join us.

In moments, the room was packed. Garrett was cradling Adam, sitting beside Carol in the center of the room. The rest were standing. Everyone, including Garrett and Carol, had a flag of a nation. We had our banners. Although most on our staff would not be accustomed to a worship tradition of loud shouting, I told them I wanted to fulfill this promise of Psalm 20 as literally and expressively as I had pictured it months earlier when first singing Adam's song. Understandably, I wondered how the staff would respond.

No one held back. The staff shouted and waved their flags joyously. Then even baby Adam, just three days old, uniquely joined in. He reached out with his tiny hand and grabbed his father's flag. Though having no idea what he was doing, infant Adam began waving his flag happily back and forth.

We had, indeed, returned to our little sanctuary where God first gave Adam's song. And God had provided the needed banners. To complete the picture, the shouts of joy came easily.

A GOOD PLACE

Although some might see all this as cute, and even curious, though still coincidental, I will always believe Adam was conceived of a song and that something of his destiny was possessed in those prophetic shouts 10 months later. There is, indeed, a possessive dimension to

> Pursuing our destiny in Christ is a continuing process of possessing God's best for our lives.

prophetic intercessory worship, which is what I believe that song and those subsequent shouts (with banners) involved.

Pursuing our destiny in Christ is a continuing process of possessing God's best for our lives. Destiny is defined as "something to which a person or thing is destined."[4] Destiny, of course, is related to the word "destination." Merriam-Webster provides the following as its first definition for destination: "The purpose for which something is destined."[5]

Recently, as Every Home for Christ was building its new international ministry headquarters, The Jericho Center, I returned again to that unusual encounter of the patriarch Jacob when the heavens were opened and he saw a stairway touching the heavens (see Gen. 28:11-22). It was during that powerfully prophetic revelation that Jacob would discover his destiny.

I was understandably drawn to this passage because of a longing to see our new ministry center embody something of Jacob's words: "What an awesome place this is! It is none other than the house of God—the gateway to heaven!" (Gen. 28:17, *NLT*).

But this time, as I reread Jacob's encounter, I noticed a phrase in the text of the *New Living Translation* that I had overlooked in previous readings. The passage says, "Meanwhile, Jacob left Beersheba and traveled toward Haran. At sundown he arrived at *a good place* to set up camp and stopped there for the night. Jacob found a stone for a pillow and lay down to sleep" (Gen. 28:10-11, *NLT*, emphasis added).

My eyes fixed on the phrase "a good place." No matter the challenges we face in our Christian walk, God can turn any tough place into a good place. For Jacob, even sleeping on a stone as he journeyed toward Haran became a good place. It was a good place because God was there.

As I thought about Jacob's "good place," several observations occurred to me regarding places awaiting us as we journey toward our destinies.

Pilgrimage

First, Jacob's good place was *a place of pilgrimage*. The Bible says, "Meanwhile, Jacob left Beersheba and traveled toward Haran" (Gen. 28:10, *NLT*). It is a simple statement, but, in a sense, a summary of Jacob's life. There were many "meanwhiles" in Jacob's journey. Jacob was a pilgrim traveling toward his God-ordained destiny. This particular stop would be for Jacob a good place, because it would be here that definition would come to his destiny.

Often it is at such stops along our own spiritual pilgrimage that clarity comes regarding God's purposes for our lives. At times we may feel as if we are sleeping on rocks, but God's presence is still with us. Each place prepares us for the rest of our pilgrimage.

Providence

Second, Jacob's good place was *a place of providence.* Jacob came to a setting where God had destined to meet him. "Providence" means "divine guidance or care."[6] Another definition reads, "God conceived as the power sustaining or guiding human destiny."[7]

> Finding our destiny is not something for which we must strive, because God's river will take us to His will.

Of this stop along Jacob's journey, the Bible tells us that Jacob "stopped there for the night. . . . As he slept, he dreamed of a stairway that reached from earth to heaven. . . . At the top of the stairway stood the LORD" (Gen. 28:11-13, *NLT*).

I believe God sets up these places of providence for His people if they will take time to wait and listen. We may not experience dramatic dreams of angelic ladders, but we can know God is there, and we can sense His guidance.

Finding our destiny is not something for which we must strive. Years ago a teenager asked me how she might find the will of God. A day earlier I had read Ezekiel's vision of a river (see Ezek. 47), and it prompted a thought. I told her, "Plunge into the river of God's Spirit and swim as deep as you can. When you surface, just rest in His presence and go with the flow. God's river will take you to His will." It may seem simplistic, but I believe it is true. God has a plan for each of us. The river of His presence will guide us.

Power

Third, Jacob's good place was *a place of power*. The patriarch experienced a supernatural power encounter as he slept on that rock. He saw into the supernatural. The text says, "As he slept, he dreamed of a stairway that reached from earth to heaven. And he saw the angels of God going up and down on it" (Gen. 28:12, *NLT*).

This is one of the more remarkable visions of Scripture. Jacob was witnessing the flow of divine activity between heaven and Earth. This experience would shape and prepare Jacob for the rest of his pilgrimage.

We, too, need God's power to reach our potential in Him. As we flow in the river of God's destiny for our lives, powerful encounters await us. We will need them from time to time. Pray much for God's power. Paul said, "For the kingdom of God is not a matter of talk but of power" (1 Cor. 4:20).

Provision

Fourth, Jacob's good place was *a place of provision*. God's first words to Jacob as he dreamt of an open heaven were, "I will give you and your descendants the land on which you are lying" (Gen. 28:13). *Jacob had been sleeping on his destiny.* The very land where he had selected his stone pillow would become the place of God's provision for His people and their destiny. It is still unfolding today!

God always provides for those who immerse themselves in Him—those who flow where His river takes them. There may be a few bends along the way, but the river knows its destination. Rest assured, it will take you to your destiny in Christ.

Promise

Fifth, Jacob's good place was *a place of promise*. The whole of Jacob's encounter involved a prophetic promise for possessing his destiny. God told Jacob, "Your descendants will be as numerous as the dust of the earth! They will cover the land from east to west and from north to south. All the families of the earth will be blessed through you and your descendants" (Gen. 28:14, *NLT*).

This was actually the continuation of a promise first given to Jacob's grandfather, Abraham. Two generations earlier God had said, "For Abraham will become a great and mighty nation, and all the nations of the earth will be blessed through him" (Gen. 18:18, *NLT*).

This Genesis passage has always had a special place in the hearts of those associated with the ministry I direct, Every Home for Christ. In 1946, when God called Jack McAlister to found this ministry, it was this passage God used to convince Jack it was possible to reach every family on Earth (right where they live) with the gospel. By 1953, in Japan, that seed would take root and bloom as the first Every Home Crusade began. At this writing, over 1 billion families (households) in 191 nations have been personally visited and given a printed presentation of a salvation message in their language.

To me, the great promise for the Church in our generation is what Christ told His disciples: "And the Good News about the Kingdom will be preached throughout the whole world, so that all nations will hear it; and then, finally, the end will come" (Matt. 24:14, *NLT*).

Compare this to what God promised Jacob regarding his descendants, "They will cover the land from east to west and from north to south" (Gen. 28:14). I believe what God is about to do through a global movement of intercessory worship and its resulting evangelism efforts will cover the whole earth with both the gospel and God's glory. God's prophecy to Isaiah will become a reality, "And as the waters fill the sea, so the earth will be filled with people who know the LORD" (Isa. 11:9, *NLT*).

Protection

Sixth, Jacob's good place was *a place of protection*. God's pledge of protection for Jacob was clearly a part of His open heaven. In addition to the promise to bless Jacob's descendants, God said, "What's more, I will be with you, and I will protect you wherever you go. . . . I will be with you constantly until I have finished giving you everything I have promised" (Gen. 28:15, *NLT*).

Here is another certainty for obedient believers: God is always near! His protection is guaranteed. In commissioning His disciples for global evangelism, Christ ended with the promise, "And be sure of this: I am with you always, even to the end of the age" (Matthew 28:20, *NLT*).

Praise

Finally, Jacob's place was *a place of praise*. It did not take long for the patriarch to realize this was no ordinary pause on the journey to his destiny. We read, "Then Jacob woke up and said, 'Surely the LORD is in this place, and I wasn't even aware of it'" (Gen. 28:16, *NLT*). Trembling with fear, Jacob adds, "What an awesome place this is! It is none other than the house of God—the gateway to heaven!" (v. 17, *NLT*).

Then, Jacob took the very stone he was sleeping on the previous night and stood it up as a memorial pillar. After pouring oil over it, he declared, "This memorial pillar will become a place for worshiping God" (v. 22, *NLT*). Amazingly, what began as a pillow—and a stone one at that—had become a pillar of praise. There is no better place to pause from time to time in our journey to God's destiny than the place of praise. Praise, to me, is the "possessive tense" of pursuing our destiny. *To praise is to prevail!*

A DREAM OF DESTINY

My wife, Dee, has an uncle, Francis Jones, who served for many years as a missionary to Kenya, East Africa. Francis grew up on a farm in northern Wisconsin and learned to "rough it" by sleeping among farm animals in a drafty barn during many cold Wisconsin winters. Francis did not think twice of using the corner of a hay bale for a pillow. He figured that farming was his destiny, just like his dad's.

But God touched the heart of Francis when he was 18 years old. Soon he was on his way to Bible college. That was in 1952. Francis ultimately became a missionary to Kenya and, during his years of tenure, became a respected professor at the East African School of Theology in Nairobi.

Although Francis loved to teach students at the seminary, he especially enjoyed those occasions when he could travel into the bush to help evangelize the lost or disciple new believers—especially those of the Massai tribe. The Massai are famous for their unique dress, most often arrayed in red, and their commitment to maintain their indigenous culture.

Francis did not mind those assignments away from the city when he had to sleep on mud floors in huts made with cow dung. Sleeping in a barn with a hay bale for a pillow had prepared him. Indeed, it brought back fond memories.

One day Francis traveled into the bush in Kenya's Narok district to teach a Massai discipleship class. About

70 attended the three day-long sessions. They sat under the shade of an old African thorn tree, some squatting in Massai fashion the entire time. For hours Francis opened God's Word and taught about Jesus.

But Francis noticed something peculiar. Off to the side, in the shadows of another tree, stood an old Massai elder listening intently to all he said. Later the missionary would learn that the man was more than 100 years old.

Though not a part of the class, the old man took in every word. He came all three days. Francis could not help but notice. As the missionary concluded that final afternoon he observed the old man coming toward him.

"Perhaps you wonder why I've stood by the tree listening to you for three days," the old man said.

Francis could understand and speak the man's language and acknowledged that he had, indeed, observed the elder. Then the old man spoke again.

"Many years ago when I was very young I had a dream. A white man came from a great distance and brought me truth about how to know God."

The old man carefully studied the features of Francis's face and added, "Your face is the face I saw in my dream."

That hot African afternoon the elderly Massai accepted Christ as his Savior. There was no mistaking his joy.

Francis realized that if the old warrior had seen his face in a dream while the man was yet young, perhaps as a teenager or younger, the missionary would not yet have been born. It reminded him of God's message to Jeremiah, "Before I formed you in the womb I knew you, before you were born I set you apart; I appointed you as a prophet to the nations" (Jer. 1:5).

Based on the old Massai's recollection of seeing the completion of Africa's East-West Railway as a youth, which Francis later learned happened in 1899, the man was probably 105 at his conversion. He lived another nine years before he went to be with Jesus.

When Francis Jones slept among those cows as a teenager in that drafty Wisconsin barn, he never could have imagined that someone in Africa had already seen his face in a dream—three decades earlier. All Francis had to do to fulfill his divine destiny was to step into this river of God's delight and go with the flow.

You may not presently see or even conceive the ultimate destiny God has planned for your life, but the river of His presence will take you there. It is God's river of your destiny. Plunge in. Swim deep. Drink freely. It is one of God's glorious rivers of delight, and intercessory worship will help you take the plunge.

Perhaps someone has even seen your face in a dream. Don't miss that divine appointment. Your destiny is waiting. *It's a good place!*

> *For the LORD your God is bringing you into a good*
> *land of flowing streams and pools of water, with*
> *springs that gush forth in the valleys and hills.*

Deuteronomy 8:7, *NLT*

ENDNOTES

Introduction
1. Darrell Patton Evans, "Let the River Flow," copyright 1995, by Mercy/Vineyard Publishing. All rights reserved. Used by permission.

Chapter One
1. Charles H. Spurgeon, *Twelve Sermons on Prayer* (Grand Rapids, MI: Baker Book House, 1971), p. 14.
2. Rick Joyner, *Shadows of Things to Come* (Nashville, TN: Thomas Nelson, Inc., 2001), pp. 95-97.
3. Jack Hayford, ed., *Spirit Filled Life Bible* (Nashville, TN: Thomas Nelson, Inc., 1991), p. 1424.
4. Ibid.
5. Jack Hayford, *Worship His Majesty* (Ventura, CA: Regal Books, 2000), p. 163.
6. Ibid.
7. Ibid.
8. Alice Smith, conversation with her husband, Eddie, Washington, DC, February 7, 2002.

Chapter Two
1. *Tibet* (Hawthorn, Victoria, Australia: Lonely Planet Publications, 2000), p. 13.
2. Paul Kyle, "Jesus We Enthrone You," copyright 1980, by Kingsway's Thankyou Music. All rights reserved. Used by permission.
3. *Fodor's Nepal, Tibet and Bhutan* (New York: Random House, 2000), p. 123.

Chapter Three
1. *Merriam-Webster's Collegiate Dictionary*, 10th ed., s.v. "intense."
2. Dick Eastman, *No Easy Road: Inspirational Thoughts on Prayer* (Grand Rapids, MI: Baker Book House, 1971), p. 109.

Chapter Five
1. *Fodor's Bali and Lombok* (New York: Random House, 2000), p. 2.
2. *Merriam-Webster's Collegiate Dictionary*, 10th ed., s.v. "perceive," "perception," "intuition."

3. Knopf Guides, *Bali*, 3rd ed. (New York: Alfred A. Knopf, 1996), p. 52.
4. John Robb, conversation with author, 1996.
5. Ibid.

Chapter Six
1. Paul DeNeui, *Missions Frontiers* (June 2001), pp. 18-19.
2. Ibid., p. 19.
3. *Merriam-Webster's Collegiate Dictionary*, 10th ed., s.v. "repent."
4. Jack Hayford, "Guarding Your Heart as a Man of Worship" (teaching presented at the Promise Keepers clergy conference, Georgia Dome, Atlanta, GA, February 14, 1996.)

Chapter Seven
1. Bible Explorer. *Theological Word Book of the Old Testament*. San Jose, CA: Epiphany Software, 1999.
2. Andrew Murray, *Humility* (New Kensington, PA: Whitaker House, 1982), p. 105.
3. Ibid., p. 6.
4. Ibid., p. 12.
5. Ibid., p. 72.
6. Ibid., p. 10.
7. Ibid., p. 37.
8. Ibid., p. 18.
9. Ibid.
10. Ibid., p. 12.
11. Ibid., p. 19.
12. Ibid., p. 56.
13. Ibid., p. 54.
14. Ibid., p. 43.
15. Ibid., p. 59.
16. Paul E. Billheimer, *Destined for the Throne* (Fort Washington, PA: Christian Literature Crusade, 1975), p. 118.

Chapter Eight
1. Bible Explorer. *Easton's Bible Dictionary*. San Jose, CA: Epiphany Software, 1999.

2. *Merriam-Webster's Collegiate Dictionary*, 10th ed., s.v. "renewal."

Chapter Nine

1. Kenneth Phillips, "One Notable Miracle" (teaching presented at the Promiseland Church, Austin, TX, June 4, 2000.)
2. Charles R. Hembree, *You and Your Money* (Grand Rapids, MI: Baker Book House, 1981), pp. 49-50.

Chapter Ten

1. Jack Hayford, *Worship His Majesty* (Ventura, CA: Regal Books, 2000), pp. 161-162.
2. Ibid., pp. 182-183.
3. Ibid., p. 185.
4. *Merriam-Webster's Collegiate Dictionary*, 10th ed., s.v. "destiny."
5. Ibid., s.v. "destination."
6. Ibid., s.v. "providence."
7. Ibid.

Every Home for Christ . . .
Reaching the Nations One Family at a Time!

Every Home for Christ, led by Dr. Dick Eastman, author of *Heights of Delight,* is a global home-to-home evangelism ministry (formerly known as World Literature Crusade) that has worked with more than 500 denominations and mission organizations to conduct Every Home Campaigns in 190 nations.

Since its inception, Every Home for Christ, with a full-time staff of over 1,200 workers plus over 2,400 volunteer associates, has distributed over 2.1 billion gospel messages home by home, resulting in over 27.5 million decision cards being mailed to EHC's numerous offices overseas and the establishing of over 43,000 village New Testament fellowships called "Christ Groups." Where illiterate people groups exist, EHC distributes gospel records and audiotapes, including the amazing "card talks" (cardboard record players). In one recent 12-month period 1,485,284 decision cards were received in EHC offices around the world, or an average of 4,069 *every day!*

To date, Every Home Campaigns have been conducted in 190 countries and completed in 90. The EHC ministry presently maintains 100 offices throughout the world, including much of the former Soviet Union and all 32 provinces and autonomous regions of China.

Because some areas of the world are virtually closed to Christian outreach, particularly in Middle Eastern countries, Every Home for Christ has developed an especially strong prayer mobilization effort through its multi-hour *Change the World School of Prayer* originated by Dick Eastman. More than 2,000,000 Christians in 120 nations have been impacted by this training, portions of which are now on DVD (video) in over 50 languages.

EHC's *Feed 5000* campaign enables believers to reach at least 5,000 people with the Gospel, over the course of a year. *Feed 5000* gives individuals a way to put feet to their prayers for the lost by providing gospel booklets and Bible-study materials that present Jesus, "the Bread of Life," for families who need to discover His offer of salvation.

Dick Eastman invites you to learn more about this opportunity by contacting Every Home for Christ for a full-color Lighthouse Edition of EHC's World Prayer Map along with information about how to become involved in feeding 5,000 the Bread of Life annually.

In the USA: Call toll-free 1-800-423-5054
Also, in the USA: 1-719-260-8888
P.O. Box 35930, Colorado Springs, CO 80935
In Canada: 1-800-265-7326
450 Speedvale Ave #101, Guelph, Ontario N1H 7X6
For other global addresses, contact EHC in the USA.
Visit our website at www.ehc.org